SPECTACULAR HOMES
of Metro New York

AN EXCLUSIVE SHOWCASE OF NEW YORK'S FINEST DESIGNERS

Published by

PANACHE
PANACHE PARTNERS, LLC

1424 Gables Court
Plano, Texas 75075
469.246.6060
Fax: 469.246.6062
www.panache.com

Publishers: Brian G. Carabet and John A. Shand
Executive Publisher: Phil Reavis
Senior Associate Publisher: Paul Geiger
Editor: Amanda Gibney Weko
Senior Designer: Emily A. Kattan
Contributing Photographer: Phillip Ennis

Printed in Malaysia

Distributed by Independent Publishers Group
800.888.4741

PUBLISHER'S DATA

Spectacular Homes of Metro New York

Library of Congress Control Number: 2007930825

ISBN 13: 978-1-933415-14-7
ISBN 10: 1-933415-14-2

First Printing 2007

10 9 8 7 6 5 4 3 2 1

Previous Page: Robin Baron Design, Inc., *page 17*
Photograph by Phillip Ennis

This Page: Geoffrey Bradfield, Inc., *page 39*
Photograph by H. Durston Saylor

SPECTACULAR HOMES
of Metro New York

AN EXCLUSIVE SHOWCASE OF NEW YORK'S FINEST DESIGNERS

FROM THE EDITOR

It has been a pleasure writing the profiles that appear within *Spectacular Homes of Metro New York*. This impressive group of design professionals brings varied levels of experience, a diverse range of aesthetics and a fascinating array of project examples, not to mention a host of awards and accolades. Yet all share a similar goal—using the power of good design to enhance the lives of their clients in a profound and positive way.

New York is undoubtedly one of the design capitals of the world. The city's unlimited resources and countless opportunities for inspiration are here for anyone to explore and embrace. For designers, the proximity to design urban lofts, beachfront cottages, country estates and mountain retreats is unlike anywhere else, and the results highlighted here are truly stunning. The collection of designers in this amazing region is also unparalleled. Legends of the profession, such as David Barrett and Geoffrey Bradfield, each with more than 40 years of experience, are featured alongside the hottest designers of today, including Jennifer Post and Eric Cohler. Up-and-coming names like Barclay Fryery and Cheryl Terrace round out the mix.

As you read about each designer's unique approach and philosophy and learn about their influences, you will note quite a bit of variety. You will also notice some common themes: a respect for, and responsibility to, the environment; a commitment to quality in materials and craftsmanship; and a passion for capturing the essence of each client's personality and lifestyle. Sometimes laugh-out-loud funny and other times quite touching, the stories are personal and endearing, and I appreciate every designer's candor and cooperation in sharing them.

I have been privileged to get to know the designers in this book, and to hear their amazing stories of creativity and success. I am now pleased to introduce them to you.

Amanda Gibney Weko

Amanda Gibney Weko

Editor

Vicente Wolf Associates, Inc., *page 271*

This introduction is meant to be the first thing you see on your journey toward witnessing breathtaking New York interior design. In reality, you have probably already wandered through *Spectacular Homes of Metro New York*. The invitation is too enticing; the anticipation is too strong. This sort of creativity demands an immediate response. In fact, each time you revisit any particular designer's work, you will undeniably see something new, perhaps an unnoticed hint of color or a sudden realization of the interplay between fabrics and furnishings. I have been viewing some of these images for months and they never cease to amaze and delight me.

My intention was to publish a beautiful book bursting with fresh images and ideas. In truth, what you are holding in your hands is a time capsule that clearly reflects our highest level of creative design. I have personally asked each designer to choose his or her favorite designs to be featured and, like most artists, his or her favorite work is almost always their latest work.

It is said that true artists see what is already there. They are the ones who make the rest of us aware of it. Great designers add yet another element to their creations. Their work must function as a part of our everyday lives, anticipate our needs and satisfy our desire for comfort. Interior designers are responsible for shaping the sanctuaries that protect us from the intrusions of the outside world. It is this intimate relationship between client and designer that produces profound and beautiful results.

Expect to be enlightened and amused by the revelations that unfold from each designer's story. You will learn what it takes to survive and thrive in the design capital of the world—passion, vision and humor.

My entire production team and I are forever grateful to the talented designers for their generosity of spirit and passion, the photographers for so brilliantly capturing the essence of each interior and the individuals who have offered us all a glimpse into their homes filled with outstanding design.

If "luck is the residue of good design," then we should all consider ourselves extraordinarily lucky to have this collection available to us. It is a fitting tribute to the great city of New York.

Paul Geiger

Paul Geiger

Senior Associate Publisher

Eric Cohler Design, *page 75*

TABLE OF CONTENTS

Brett Design, Inc., *page 31*

Christopher Maya, Inc., *page 193*

Randall A. Ridless, LLC, *page 241*

Sussan Lari Architect PC, *page 175*

"The best designers can create, at every level, an element of the unexpected."

—Mark Alan Polo

Eric Cohler Design, *page 75*

NEW YORK

JIM AMAN
ANNE CARSON

AMAN & CARSON, INC.

A professionally designed room can dramatically impact all who view it. The process of installing an interior design, on the contrary, often seems anti-climactic. After months of planning, purchasing and preparations, the final scene is usually assembled and styled in a piecemeal fashion, as construction is finished and furnishings are delivered. The design team of Jim Aman and Anne Carson never let lead times obstruct the full impact of their glamorous and elegant interiors. Their designs are always installed and styled in a single, carefully organized event. Taking cues from their background as store designers for Ralph Lauren, the two understand the excitement of presenting a complete composition to their clients, with whom they work closely to create highly personalized and polished homes.

"What we're good at is listening to our clients, and blending their lifestyle, architecture and location," explains Anne. The designers' portfolio has a traditional flavor, what they call "updated, classic American design." Serene, neutral palettes are accented with the unexpected—such as an Hermès scarf-covered pillow or custom furniture. Superior workmanship from a range of top-of-the-line resources is one of the firm's hallmarks. Comfort and livability are always held in high regard.

Jim Aman is a graduate of the Pratt Institute. He began his career working at Polo Ralph Lauren Corp. developing all of the visual aspects of the Polo environment, from contributing to the design of the flagship Manhattan store to creating designs for personal residences for the Lauren family. Prior to founding Aman & Carson in 1994, he also developed store identity concepts for Wathne Limited.

ABOVE
The corner of the living room boasts a stunning limestone mantelpiece and a flame-crotch paneled mahogany wall.
Photograph by Ricky Zehavi

FACING PAGE
The amazing Manhattan views provide a backdrop for this streamlined, elegantly designed living room. Exotic touches of animal print, a fur throw and mica-covered coffee tables add to the overall glamour.
Photograph by Ricky Zehavi

Anne Carson earned a Bachelor of Science in marketing from Lehigh University and a Certificate of Interior Design from Parsons School of Design. She also spent her early career working at Polo Ralph Lauren Corp. developing designs for the flagship Manhattan store and other locations around the world. Designing the showrooms and styling advertising sets for the brand's home collection taught her how to perfect details.

Jim and Anne share a passion for fine materials and elegant traditional details; they also share a desire to create spaces for real people. They left behind careers designing rooms purely for aesthetic appeal and began Aman & Carson to create houses that are both beautiful and functional. "There is much more gratitude now because we can see our clients enjoy what we design," explains Anne. "We always take into consideration that long after we are gone, people live there."

Aman & Carson's work has been featured in *Architectural Digest, House Beautiful, Florida Design* and *Town and Country.* Among other awards, the firm was cited as one of 12 designers making significant contributions to design and architecture by The Decoration and Design Building.

MORE ABOUT JIM & ANNE ...

WHAT ONE ELEMENT OF STYLE OR PHILOSOPHY HAVE YOU STUCK
WITH FOR YEARS THAT STILL WORKS FOR YOU TODAY?

Jim: To never follow trends.

Anne: Glamour; when you add it, people feel special.

WHAT IS THE MOST UNIQUE/IMPRESSIVE/BEAUTIFUL HOME YOU
HAVE EVER SEEN?

Jim: Beauport in Gloucester, MA.

Anne: The Rockefeller Mansion in Greenwich; it is a like a time capsule of authenticity.

WHAT SINGLE THING WOULD BRING A DULL HOUSE TO LIFE?

Jim: Painting a room can give you a whole new life.

Anne: Plants and flowers liven up any room.

WHAT CAN WE FIND YOU DOING WHEN YOU ARE
NOT DESIGNING?

Jim: Listening to my iPod.

Anne: Spending time with my three kids.

AMAN & CARSON, INC.
Jim Aman, ASID
Anne Carson, ASID
19 West 55th Street
New York, NY 10019
212.247.7577
www.amancarson.com

ROBIN BARON
ROBIN BARON DESIGN, INC.

R obin Baron, founder of Robin Baron Design, Inc., brings more than beauty to the homes she designs. She brings comfort, livability and a sense of calm to the lives of her clients. "I enjoy helping people live more positively by influencing their surroundings," she relates. The ability to impact people in a beneficial way is what drew Robin to interior design. She begins each project with a process that allows her to "get into her clients' heads," taking clients shopping to see which colors, textures, patterns and furnishings elicit response, and then interpreting what that means for their homes. "My philosophy is to understand my clients and see things through their perspective," Robin says. "This enables me to create a home that is distinctly their own."

Clients trust Robin to think outside the box. The level of trust she establishes over the course of a project ensures the client will take the leap of faith required to create their unique home. Known for developing strong personal relationships, Robin inspires her clients with the same enthusiasm for design that she, herself, exudes. From traditional to contemporary, formal to casual, every home should capture the spirit, energy and lifestyle of the client, she believes.

"The most challenging projects are the most rewarding," says Robin, who works most often on interiors that include construction and renovation. She advocates bringing an interior designer on board early in the process, so that a home's architecture merges seamlessly with the decorating concepts. Based in New York, Robin's eight-person firm has completed projects along the East Coast and across the country.

Robin's diverse background infuses her work with a variety of creative inspirations. Having attended Parsons School of Design and UCLA for both fashion and interior design, Robin has been a fashion designer with her own label.

ABOVE
To create drama in the foyer to a master bedroom suite, Robin hung an antique mirror she found in a French chateau.
Photograph by Phillip Ennis

FACING PAGE
Robin highlights this airy music room in Westchester, New York, with simple yet beautiful drapery panels and a custom rug. This sets the stage for the piano and antique harp, played by the client's daughter.
Photograph by Phillip Ennis

An interior designer and owner of her own firm for the past 17 years, Robin is active professionally as an allied member of the American Society of Interior Designers (ASID), the International Interior Design Association, the International Furnishings & Design Association and the Women Presidents Organization.

"I pride myself on not having a pre-determined 'Robin Baron' look," she explains, adding that each project is about the individual client's needs, loves and dreams. Robin complements each client's personality with an eclectic mix of design details. Good design is about these details, ensuring finished rooms that are balanced and use juxtapositions that are in harmony. "Livable homes are my trademark," says the designer who has literally trademarked the term. Each project is a reflection of the client, and a place where he or she can relax and feel comfortable within beautiful surroundings. In short, Robin Baron homes are ones you never want to leave.

MORE ABOUT ROBIN ...

WHAT WOULD YOUR FRIENDS TELL US ABOUT YOU?

I am optimistic, energetic and outgoing.

IF YOU COULD ELIMINATE ONE DESIGN STYLE FROM THE WORLD, WHAT WOULD IT BE?

Design is about inspiration and I am inspired by many different—and sometimes unexpected—styles and techniques, so I wouldn't eliminate any one style.

WHAT IS THE HIGHEST COMPLIMENT YOU'VE RECEIVED PROFESSIONALLY?

A client recently told me that I was more than a designer, and that I was more like a life coach for her during the project. The same client's 17-year-old daughter, who hadn't seen the furnishings in the new home until they were completely installed, cried the first time she saw the interiors because she felt they were so beautiful.

ROBIN BARON DESIGN, INC.
Robin Baron, Allied Member, ASID
1776 Broadway, Suite 1006
New York, NY 10019
212.262.1110
www.robinbarondesign.com

DAVID BARRETT
DAVID BARRETT INTERIOR DESIGN

One of the most well-respected and renowned interior designers practicing today, David Barrett, FASID, has more than a half-century of design experience to reflect upon. A graduate of L'École Nationale des Beaux Arts in Paris, David began his namesake design practice in New York in 1950. "It has never been about what's chic," he says. "Interior design is about working with people. You must always put something of the client's personality into a room. That's what will be timeless and appropriate." David's industry tenure affords him great perspective and keeps him grounded in two key principles: Every one of his jobs is handled individually based upon the relationship with the client and every design is different. As such, he has completed projects for generations of families and worked in locales as diverse as California, Texas, Florida, and Maine, as well as the greater New York metropolitan area.

Whether the project is a house, an apartment, a yacht or a restaurant, David and his staff of six put the same intensive amount of thought into creating spaces that are highly personalized and comfortable. "Rooms have to have some excitement," David explains of designs that never look staid or typical, but instead offer a touch of humor and fantasy. His use of trompe l'oeil, mirror and playful patterns—monkeys are a common imagery—imbue rooms with a mix of period aesthetics he calls "Salade Niçoise" style. Incorporating these touches of whimsy and supporting the preferences of his clients ensures David's projects are always apropos. "A design I completed 30 years ago still looks good today," he describes, simply because it fits the family with both style and originality.

The work of David Barrett has been featured in *Architectural Digest*, *House Beautiful*, *House & Garden*, *Interior Design* and *The New York Times*. In 1972, David was advanced to Fellowship in the American Society of Interior Designers. He has served as president of the organization's New York chapter. Today, David continues to enjoy the artistic side of his practice. He also maintains active involvement in a variety of designer philanthropies, including the Kips Bay Decorator Showhouse; 2007 marked the 35th anniversary of his participation and the 10th anniversary that he created a room for the organization.

John Miller, a longtime employee of the firm, describes David's collaborative nature with his staff and clients: "David's twist on things is the reason for his success. He introduces and completes concepts and gives clients more than the average designer because he listens. His way of elaborating on a client's ideas is unique."

TOP LEFT
The family gathers here informally for a panoramic view of the dunes and ocean. The swag window treatments are faux painted because any fabric would fade, due to the strong reflection of the sun. The corner topiary with shelves is in keeping with the trompe l'oeil theme.
Photograph by Bill Rothchild

BOTTOM LEFT
The Louis XV Boiserie paneling is accessorized with an antique Moroccan mirror, bronze four-arm appliqués and several 18th- and 19th-century architectural models. A Directoire lit de repos anchors the opposite wall. A Louis XVI table in the center acts as a dining table for intimate dinners and rests on an Aubusson carpet.
Photograph by Bill Rothchild

FACING PAGE LEFT
Red lacquered walls and the red stained floor create a background for the 19th-century black wood and mother of pearl opium bed, which is flanked by a pair of Lalique consoles. In the foreground is a 19th-century root table, bench and eight-arm Swedish crystal chandelier.
Photograph by Bill Rothchild

FACING PAGE RIGHT
A fantasy ruins mural creates the background for this Palm Beach dining room. A granite pedestal supports the glass-top dining table and is flanked by Louis XV side chairs. The 19th-century chandelier is made of crystal and bronze.
Photograph by Bill Rothchild

MORE ABOUT DAVID ...

WHAT ONE ELEMENT OF STYLE OR PHILOSOPHY HAVE YOU STUCK
WITH FOR YEARS THAT STILL WORKS FOR YOU TODAY?

Comfort with a touch of humor and fantasy.

IF YOU COULD ELIMINATE ONE DESIGN STYLE FROM THE WORLD,
WHAT WOULD IT BE?

Minimalism; it lacks personality.

WHAT BOOK HAS HAD THE GREATEST IMPACT ON YOU?

The Bible.

WHAT IS THE MOST UNIQUE/IMPRESSIVE/BEAUTIFUL HOME YOU'VE
SEEN AND WHY?

Villa Trianon, Versailles, France; the home of Elsie De Wolfe, for its perfection of design,
fantasy and furniture of the period. Or, Gertrude Stein's home in Paris, filled with the
paintings and possessions she loves.

DAVID BARRETT INTERIOR DESIGN
David Barrett, FASID
131 East 71st Street
New York, NY 10021
212.585.3180
www.davidbarrettinteriors.com

LISA BARTOLOMEI
BARTOLOMEI AND COMPANY

Lisa Bartolomei, founder of the design firm Bartolomei and Company, practiced commercial interior design concentrating on a variety of projects, including restaurants, hotels, banks, retail stores, law offices and health facilities for 10 years before making the move to residential interiors. Her strong desire to make an impact on individuals' lives led her to create the firm in 1986 and she has been improving her clients' lives ever since. She is committed to helping people find happiness in their homes and making interior spaces work for them, and her keen artistic eye and design expertise blossom with each project she completes.

"I make it about them," Lisa says. "Design is all about my clients." Lisa's incredible ability to listen has given her the reputation as the designer who "listens between the lines." Making every effort to get to know her clients before launching the design process, she goes through image after image with her clients, accompanies them on shopping trips and spends time talking with them to ascertain what they love and also what they hate about different aspects of design. She also works strictly within her clients' budgets with a keen understanding that design priorities shift on a client-to-client basis. Her innate ability to listen, coupled with her intuitive understanding

of client needs, enables her to convey what her clients want before they can conceive it themselves.

Lisa prefers that her work reflect who the client is and not who the designer is.

"I want each of my clients' homes to look as if they have been collecting things over a lifetime, not as if a designer has just stepped in to make things perfect." Like a detective, she gathers every bit of information possible to determine how her clients like to live and then she uses her expertise to create a better lifestyle for them.

ABOVE
The soft greens and browns used in this dining room help to bring the outside in, no matter the time of year.
Photograph by Geoffrey Hodgdon

FACING PAGE
This family room is a study in textures and neutrals. Exotic touches—such as the 1960s' glazed terracotta Italian lamp and the antique Moroccan table—reflect the diverse taste of this well-traveled resident.
Photograph by Geoffrey Hodgdon

Lisa truly enjoys the problem-solving element of design and often creates custom pieces of furniture as well as redesigns the architectural elements within the spaces, giving her clients unique, comfortable, beautiful and highly usable environments. She masterfully unearths the lifestyle her clients envisage for themselves–whether consciously or subconsciously. Rather than just decorating, it is her goal to create a total environment for each client.

In order to offer extremely personalized interiors, Lisa goes on buying trips to London, Paris, Venice, New York, Atlanta, New Orleans and numerous cities in California to provide her clients with unique furnishings and artwork at excellent prices. While based

in Washington, D.C., her work reaches the global scale; she has completed projects in Jordan, Paris, Bermuda, New York City, The Hamptons, San Francisco, Florida and

ABOVE LEFT
A soothing haven in off-whites and chalky blue, the master bedroom is adorned with fabrics and carpet which are made of linen, adding to the relaxed feeling of the room.
Photograph by Geoffrey Hodgdon

ABOVE RIGHT
The antique painted Indian screen adds a delicate yet exotic flavor.
Photograph by Geoffrey Hodgdon

FACING PAGE
This beach house living room is filled with a mixture of antique and modern elements. The lamps are plaster from the 1950s, as is the root-wood coffee table with a kidney-shaped top. The use of floral linen for the draperies continues the garden feeling.
Photograph by Geoffrey Hodgdon

numerous residences in the Washington, D.C., area. As Bartolomei and Company grows, so does its reach; Lisa has been featured in the pages of numerous publications, including *Interior Design* magazine, *The Washington Post* and on the screens of televisions across the country on "Good Morning America" and ABC News with John Harter.

MORE ABOUT LISA ...

WHAT THINGS WOULD YOU DO TO BRING A DULL HOUSE TO LIFE?

Making better use of color, architectural focal points, window structure and lighting are sure to bring a dull house to life.

WHO HAS HAD THE BIGGEST INFLUENCE ON YOUR CAREER?

Helene Giafferi, a friend of mine and dealer of fine art in Paris. She took me by the hand and led me through homes and auction houses in Europe, educating my eye for design.

WHAT IS YOUR GREATEST PERSONAL INDULGENCE?

Travel; I love Italy and France and I couldn't live without New York. It is a place like no other and a virtual candy store for any designer.

HAVE YOU BEEN PUBLISHED IN ANY NATIONAL OR REGIONAL PUBLICATIONS?

Yes, my work has been featured on the cover of *Country Inns* and in the pages of the *Washington Business Journal*, *Washington Post Magazine*, *Washingtonian Magazine*, *Style*, *Interior Design*, *Home & Design Magazine*, *Chesapeake Home* and *Washington Spaces Magazine*.

BARTOLOMEI AND COMPANY
Lisa Bartolomei
202.965.7667
Fax: 202.338.5221
www.bartolomeiandcompany.com

BRETT BELDOCK

BRETT DESIGN, INC.

Just as a couture suit jacket might have an unexpectedly playful pattern on its lining, interiors designed by Brett Beldock of Brett Design, Inc. always feature elements of surprise and delight. The Parsons-educated Brett spent 10 years as a fashion designer before a friend asked her for help decorating a townhouse. Brett realized her true calling and has owned and operated her own interior design practice since 1988. Qualities derived from her fashion background, including finesse with color and texture, have defined her portfolio of custom residential work.

Brett favors unexpected pairings—such as Queen Anne chairs upholstered in patent leather or an iridescent garden stool alongside a Ruhlmann or Adenet chair from the 1940s—and explains that these offer the element of fun. "I always try to retain my sense of humor—we're not dealing with blood plasma," she laughs. The self-described "architectural junkie" is able to play with design because she is so well-versed in architectural history.

Brett is a licensed New York State contractor, and much of her business is design-build. She views each client's project in much the same way she used to envision a new clothing collection: with a fresh eye. The interaction is close, with a lot of

feedback from both sides. Brett listens to how her clients want to live, and then does her best to intuit what they want. Each project looks clearly different, yet has a crisp and clean aesthetic, often accented by Brett's own custom furniture designs. She acknowledges the importance of designing homes to reflect lifestyles, but adds "the process should be enjoyable."

Equally significant to Brett's work is the give-and-take that comes from teaching. She teaches at New York University—which bestowed upon her the Excellence in Service Award for 15 years of teaching—and New York Institute of Technology.

She has also served as a juror at Parsons School of Design and Yale School of Architecture. While she shares her own experiences and approach with future designers, she also gains the fresh insights her students have to offer. The youthful energy infuses her work and reminds her that "every room should sparkle."

Brett Design, Inc. is particularly excited about design-build projects that are Green and environmentally safe. The company is working on a home in Naples, Florida, which will be built with ecologically friendly building products, reclaimed timber flooring and reclaimed glass. The fabrics and carpets in each room will be made of environmentally safe cottons and natural banana leaf bamboo and silk. The company is working on two assisted living facilities which will also be eco-friendly.

Brett has brought variety and fresh spontaneity to most of the major decorators' showhouses, and has been featured recently in the *New York Times*, *Home*, *Hampton Cottages & Gardens* and in 10 books.

MORE ABOUT BRETT...

WHAT ONE ELEMENT OF STYLE OR PHILOSOPHY HAVE YOU STUCK
WITH FOR YEARS THAT STILL WORKS FOR YOU TODAY?
I impress upon clients to buy only the things they really love. If you are true to yourself,
you'll always be happy.

IF YOU COULD ELIMINATE ONE DESIGN/ARCHITECTURAL/BUILDING
TECHNIQUE OR STYLE FROM THE WORLD, WHAT WOULD IT BE?
1950s' furniture.

WHAT DO YOU LIKE BEST ABOUT PRACTICING IN NEW YORK?
The world is our oyster; I like the option to always take a tour or a course, visit a
museum or just walk around different areas of the city for inspiration. There are always
opportunities to keep getting ideas.

WHO HAS HAD THE BIGGEST INFLUENCE ON YOUR CAREER?
Le Corbusier and John Saladino.

BRETT DESIGN, INC.
Brett Beldock
201 East 87th Street
New York, NY 10128
212.987.8270
www.brettdesigninc.com

Bruce Bierman
BRUCE BIERMAN DESIGN, INC.

At the age of four, Bruce Bierman accompanied his family into a neighbor's home, promptly telling the homeowner her drapes were all wrong. His family jokes they always knew Bruce would go into design; a childhood spent playing with Legos, drawing floor plans and critiquing the décor of others was clear evidence of his creative spirit. Today, the Interior Design Hall of Famer has more than 30 years of professional interior design experience to his credit, and a portfolio of work where spatial psychology and aesthetic beauty are employed in harmonious tandem.

"I want a client to walk into a space and sigh—a sigh of pleasure," Bruce describes. His subtle use of psychology, and intuitive understanding of how people resonate emotionally within spaces, stems from his education. Two degrees from the Rhode Island School of Design—one in fine art and another in architecture—provide very different design perspectives. Generally speaking, architecture training is based upon solving problems and working within functionality parameters, while art education emphasizes aesthetic exploration of materials, forms and colors. Bruce's art background inspired his appreciation for fine craftsmanship as well as technical

expertise with materials ranging from textiles to wood. His architecture education offers the pragmatic planning skills to keep his interiors not only beautiful but ultimately liveable.

Bruce's opportunity at RISD is always influencing what he describes as the "back-and-forth swings" of design. The super-organized designer is attentive to every detail, emphasizing appropriate proportions above all else. He understands the importance of placing lighting within reading areas, incorporating ample storage space and accommodating individual body sizes within spaces that look and feel comfortable. His aesthetic tendencies run toward natural materials, visually soothing color schemes and spaces that are warm and inviting, without seeming showy or contrived.

ABOVE
Overlooking Central Park, this living room has a Ruhlmann-inspired chaise as well as a parchment and mahogany cabinet in the style of Jean-Michel Frank to hide audio-visual components.
Photograph courtesy of Bruce Bierman Design

FACING PAGE
The library windows have Venetian wood blinds. Geometrically patterned, the rug supplies the room's color palette. The game table and coffee table are in the style of Jean-Michel Frank.
Photograph courtesy of Bruce Bierman Design

Bruce founded his namesake firm in 1977. Today, Bruce Bierman Design, Inc. includes 20 staff members. Widely published and highly regarded, the firm and its work have been featured in *Elle Décor*, *New York Magazine*, *The Robb Report*, *Esquire* and others, as well as magazines in Europe, Japan and South America. *House Beautiful* recently named Bruce one of "America's Most Brilliant Decorators A-Z" and "One of the Top Ten Designers to Watch." The firm actively engages its clients in the process, taking them beyond what they might have expected. In doing so, they attain Bruce's ideal for great designers: "Our role is to help clients realize their own personal style."

ABOVE
The bedroom and dining room have panoramic views of Central Park. Folding laminated glass panels are framed with mahogany.
Photograph courtesy of Bruce Bierman Design

FACING PAGE
Dominated by a 19th-century dog painting, the living room is designed for flexibility in uses: Chairs are on casters and the coffee table contains a hidden television projector. Club chairs are styled in the manner of Jean-Michel Frank.
Photograph courtesy of Bruce Bierman Design

MORE ABOUT BRUCE...

WHAT IS THE BEST PART OF BEING AN INTERIOR DESIGNER?

One of my clients wrote me a letter: "I am so happy in my house ... it is like falling in love; I can't sleep, eat or think about anything else. Thank you for making this happen." Seeing my designs come to life and having clients who feel their expectations have been far exceeded is the best part of my work.

WHAT IS THE HIGHEST COMPLIMENT YOU'VE RECEIVED PROFESSIONALLY?

Being inducted into the Interior Design Hall of Fame in 2000. Since I began my career, I have always admired the creative work done by previous inductees. Being nominated by these same professionals, and knowing they are aware of my work, has been the highest career compliment.

WHAT DO YOU LIKE BEST ABOUT PRACTICING IN YOUR LOCALE?

New York City is a magnet for some of the most interesting and successful people in the world. Living here has given me the opportunity to meet and work with some of them.

WHEN YOU ARE NOT WORKING WHAT CAN YOU BE FOUND DOING?

Playing with my dog, Rocky, a Dandy Dinmont Terrier.

BRUCE BIERMAN DESIGN, INC.
Bruce Bierman
29 West 15th Street, Ninth Floor
New York, NY 10011
212.243.1935
www.biermandesign.com

GEOFFREY BRADFIELD

GEOFFREY BRADFIELD, INC.

You might think that after four decades as a designer, Geoffrey Bradfield would be resting on his laurels, content to keep things status quo. Think again. The trendsetting interior designer continues to set precedents in creativity as well as practice. Geoffrey has a great respect for "our moment in time," emphasizing contemporary design, contemporary art and an ever-present search for new challenges within design projects and around the globe. His firm, Geoffrey Bradfield, Inc., recently opened companies in Dubai in the United Arab Emirates and in Qatar. Another satellite office is located in Palm Beach. The firm's brand of "functional opulence" reinterprets design cues from the 1930s, infusing them with contemporary materials and artwork, for a truly 21st-century aesthetic.

No matter how technology may change, Geoffrey always emphasizes the basic desire for comfort all of his clients seek. "If we forget comfort, we miss the point of home," he explains. His stylish designs are tailored carefully to the lifestyles of the occupants. While comfort is paramount, the eclectic exuberance displayed by Geoffrey's work stems from the incorporation of fine artwork. "Even the most staid room gains vigor from contemporary art," Geoffrey believes. His own passion for collecting invariably

extends to his clients. This combination ultimately makes his interiors luxurious as well as livable.

Geoffrey remains very hands-on in most projects, but he is quick to credit the creativity and intelligence of his 12-person staff, including associate designer Roric Tobin. "I like to surround myself with positive-thinking people," he explains in his soft British accent, adding that he hopes his own attitude of optimism sets the office tone. Born in South Africa, Geoffrey received his design training working around the globe. He was also a partner of the late Jay Spectre. Since founding his own firm in the United States in 1992, Geoffrey has been continuously earning recognition— and clients—for his timeless modern interiors.

ABOVE
Classical allusions flank either side of the sleek entrance hall: a contemporary bronze sculpture, *Hermes*, by Sabin Howard and a historical photomural of the townhouse façade in the 1940s.
Photograph by H. Durston Saylor

FACING PAGE
In the living room, a dramatically carved custom rug anchors clear acrylic pieces from Geoffrey's Millennium Modern furniture collection. Artwork by Francois-Xavier Lalanne, Sophia Vari, Joel Perlman and Rachel Hovnanian. The custom fabricated fireplace, imported from England, was the first of its kind in the States.
Photograph by H. Durston Saylor

While Geoffrey has worked for world-famous clients, he is not one to name-drop. "Our clients are very private, and we respect that privacy," he describes. The firm has even coined the term "silent celebrities" to refer to this list. Although client names may not always be revealed, Geoffrey Bradfield, Inc. gets its share of publicity. The firm's work has been profiled in *Elle Décor*, *Interior Design*, *Metropolitan Home* and on the CNN and HGTV television networks. Geoffrey has been included four times on the *Architectural Digest* "AD 100" list of the world's top designers, and has been named one of the magazine's top 30 "Deans of American Design." The book *Geoffrey Bradfield: Defining Millennium Modern*, illustrating his elegantly modern designs, debuted in 2004.

MORE ABOUT GEOFFREY...

WHAT BOOK ARE YOU READING RIGHT NOW?

The Essence of Style by Joan DeJean.

WHAT ONE PHILOSOPHY HAVE YOU STUCK WITH FOR YEARS THAT STILL WORKS FOR YOU TODAY?

When in doubt, don't.

WHAT SINGLE THING WOULD YOU DO TO BRING A DULL HOUSE TO LIFE?

Add glamour through the use of mirror; it introduces a sense of infinity and grandeur.

WHAT IS THE HIGHEST COMPLIMENT YOU'VE RECEIVED PROFESSIONALLY?

In 2005, I was recognized by *Architectural Digest* as a Dean of American Design.

GEOFFREY BRADFIELD, INC.
Geoffrey Bradfield
116 East 61st Street
New York, NY 10021
212.758.1773
www.geoffreybradfield.com

BENJAMIN W. BRADLEY
DAVID THIERGARTNER

BRADLEY THIERGARTNER INTERIORS

It is not often that two people meet professionally who share the identical design philosophy, approach and creative passions. However, that is just the case with principals Benjamin Bradley and David Thiergartner of Bradley Thiergartner Interiors. Their unique collaborative relationship with each other and with their clients is the strength of their firm's award-winning work. They call their style "Tailored Traditionalism" but it is more about a permeable sense of integrity and aesthetic sophistication than any definable style. Elegant and comfortable interiors are highly personalized for each client's lifestyle, with color palettes rich in vibrant warmth. "Our projects are about taking a client's personal style and creating an interior that suits them, their location and the architecture of their home," Benjamin explains.

"We want to provide our clients with homes they are proud of," explains David. The two principals are most interested in balancing function with beauty, and pride themselves on how well they listen to what clients truly want and need. "Quality is the underlying basis for everything we do," adds Benjamin. From fine fabrics to high-end furniture and antiques, the firm's choices are about bringing a warm,

inviting feeling to every home. In the firm's 13-year history, completed projects across the country show the pair's creative range across geography as varied as Midtown Manhattan, Scottsdale, Arizona, and the coasts of Nantucket, California and Florida.

Benjamin and David both bring creative backgrounds to their work. Benjamin has an education in fashion and textile design, while David studied music extensively at various institutions. Their collective backgrounds, as well as a keen understanding of color, scale and proportion, are brought to every project. "When you have an established and ongoing appreciation for art, music or fashion, your interests in all things creative can translate to any medium, interiors included," Benjamin explains.

ABOVE
An antique model ship alludes to the home's beachside locale.
Photograph by Phillip Ennis

FACING PAGE
Post-and-beam construction, traditional furnishings and contemporary artwork lend an air of relaxed sophistication to this living space.
Photograph by Phillip Ennis

Today, Benjamin and David gain inspiration from the clients with whom they work and the city around them. Every cab ride or walk down a New York street is an opportunity for new ideas. "There is incredible beauty around us," says David. Benjamin adds, "There are unexpected spaces behind every apartment building façade; you never know what type of space the elevator is going to open upon." Chances are, whatever project the two encounter will be enhanced by their creative elegance, style and grace.

TOP LEFT
An antique rug inspired the color scheme of this Art Deco-influenced influenced living room. Parchment covers the walls.
Photograph by Phillip Ennis

BOTTOM LEFT
An original Tiffany Studios "Magnolia" floor lamp provided additional color inspiration. The firm designed the custom fireplace surround; the gold leaf settee is by Jacque Ruhlmann.
Photograph by Phillip Ennis

FACING PAGE
This living room, although traditionally inspired, resides in a loft in Soho, New York. A collection of Royal Copenhagen pottery, a Japanese bronze lamp and works of art by Frankenthaler and Thiebault add elegance to this former industrial space.
Photograph by Phillip Ennis

MORE ABOUT BENJAMIN & DAVID ...

WHO HAS HAD THE BIGGEST INFLUENCE ON YOUR CAREERS?

Mrs. Susan Weber Soros, founder and director of the Bard Center for Graduate Studies in New York. As an early client who really enjoyed the design process, she was a mentor and source of encouragement.

WHAT SINGLE THING WOULD YOU DO TO BRING A DULL HOUSE TO LIFE?

Benjamin: Add music or fresh flowers; a house can be technically beautiful, but isn't complete without a sense of life.

WHAT ONE PHILOSOPHY HAVE YOU STUCK WITH FOR YEARS THAT STILL WORKS FOR YOU TODAY?

David: Integrity; it applies to the quality of fabric or furniture and the appropriateness and authenticity of architectural details.

WHEN YOU ARE NOT DESIGNING, WHERE CAN YOU BE FOUND?

Benjamin: Scouring flea markets, reading or antiquing.

David: In my garden.

BRADLEY THIERGARTNER INTERIORS
Benjamin W. Bradley
David Thiergartner
183 Madison Avenue, Suite 904
New York, NY 10016
212.779.1717
www.bradleythiergartnerinteriors.com

BRIAN P. BRADY

BRADY DESIGN, INC.

Tucked amidst the trendy retailers in Southampton, New York, is the showroom and design office of Brian P. Brady. With his classical background and international training, Brian clearly illustrates what timeless design is all about. He is both a registered architect and an interior designer, specializing in casually elegant residential designs. Brian Brady Design, Inc. is sought out by clients seeking its signature look, which emphasizes natural materials, abundant light and a sense of livable comfort.

Brian attended the University of Notre Dame where he earned a Bachelor of Architecture degree in 1978. He then spent a year studying the tenets of classical architecture in Rome, infusing his work with strong lines, clean symmetry and human proportions. Brian's professional experience has taken him worldwide, including Greece, Singapore and Paris. His tenure with the internationally acclaimed architecture firm of I.M. Pei & Partners brought him large-scale experience designing art and cultural facilities. After completing several freelance residential projects, Brian founded his namesake firm in 1989 to pursue residential design full-time. "I love the personal interaction of working with clients and becoming close friends," he explains of his decision to leave large-scale architecture behind.

Since the firm's inception, client involvement has remained a priority. At the start of a project, Brian prefers that clients come prepared with photos and ideas of what they like. He will often take this information and conceptualize a design before a proposal is even signed, to ensure everyone is speaking the same design language when the project begins.

Brian sketches constantly, and reads and travels extensively for inspiration. His creativity on projects extends from architecture to interiors to furniture design. Working with a 90-year-old, family-owned furniture workroom in Pennsylvania, Brian designs all of the upholstered pieces he incorporates into projects. This allows him to specify the size, shape and amount and type of fill, so that the pieces are tailored to the room and family who will use them.

ABOVE
Flat paneling was added to the entry hall of a Southampton, New York, turn-of-the-century farmhouse to give the space a quiet formality.
Photograph by Eric Striffler

FACING PAGE
This Southampton, New York, living room hints of the ocean with its cerulean-blue sofa crisply piped in white. The tailored lines of the pieces are at once traditional and modern.
Photograph by Eric Striffler

The work of Brady Design has been featured in *House Beautiful, Interior Design, House & Garden* and *Hamptons Cottages & Gardens*. In 2007, Brian served as design director for the Hamptons Cottages & Gardens Idea House, which is located in Amagansett, New York. He and partner Franco Biscardi will also be designing the living room in the classic Shingle-style residence. Brian is also an avid squash player and has been engaged in pro bono design services for the expansion of a local recreation center and the creation of a public squash center containing four singles courts and a doubles court. He is also helping the organization develop a junior squash program for underprivileged children.

MORE ABOUT BRIAN ...

ON WHAT PERSONAL INDULGENCE DO YOU SPEND THE
MOST MONEY?

Travel; I go to Italy as often as I can.

WHO HAS HAD THE BIGGEST INFLUENCE ON YOUR CAREER?

I.M. Pei; he influenced my detailing, not as a Modernist, but in terms of conceiving a
project where everything is well thought out.

IF YOU COULD ELIMINATE ONE DESIGN/ARCHITECTURAL/BUILDING
TECHNIQUE OR STYLE FROM THE WORLD, WHAT WOULD IT BE?

Post-modernism.

WHAT IS THE BEST PART OF BEING A DESIGNER?

The fact that you are creating an environment from a thought.

BRADY DESIGN, INC.
Brian P. Brady, AIA
22 Main Street
Southampton, NY 11968
631.283.3111
www.bbradydesign.com

TERE BRESIN

BERET DESIGN GROUP, INC.

Designer Tere Bresin is always ready to celebrate life. She looks for any excuse for a gathering, believing that sharing your home with family and friends is critical to happiness. Naturally, the interior designer brings this passion for living to every home she designs. Working with their unique personalities, Tere helps clients create their own distinct looks, emphasizing luxurious materials, layered lighting and a sense of order and balance. "Life is short; your home should be the best place in the world to be," she believes.

Following a period of time in commercial design, Tere founded Beret Design Group, Inc. in 1993. The firm completes a mix of residential and commercial projects, including offices, restaurants and spas. Residences have varied in size from small urban apartments to grand coastline estates. "My best projects have been team efforts," Tere describes. She is known for collaborating with her clients as well as technical consultants and other design professionals with whom she works. Accessibility for an aging population, environmental responsibility and the way spaces change use over time are important considerations to her.

Tere earned a Bachelor of Fine Arts degree—and spent some time as a fine arts teacher—before transitioning to interior design. She credits the art background with allowing her to visualize projects in terms of form, line, color and texture. The perspective gives her a sense of balance between the beautiful and practical sides of design.

One of the tenets of Tere's approach is the absence of "standout" elements. Instead, she likes a cohesive environment that offers the initial "wow" factor without distractions. She wants people to slowly absorb all of the details of a space, from the texture of a sofa to the pattern on a drapery fabric. "I want a room to feel good as an experience." She adds that incorporating sound, scent and visual comfort to an interior can engage all of the senses in a positive way.

Tere is a member of the American Society of Interior Designers, and has served as president of the New Jersey chapter. She is National Council for Interior Design Qualification (NCIDQ) certified. She has been selected to participate in the Montclair Designer Showhouse and the Designer Showhouse of New Jersey as well as the Women's Association of Morristown Memorial Hospital's "Mansion in May." Her work has received numerous awards, including several ASID Gold Awards of Excellence. As a participant on the HGTV hit show "Designer's Challenge," Tere was the designer selected to create a new dining room and foyer. Beret Design Group and its projects have also been featured in *House Beautiful, DesignNJ, Savvy Living, NJ Monthly* and *New York Spaces.*

TOP LEFT
An elegant and sophisticated mélange of fine art, including a Robert Kelly triptych, is beautifully balanced by the subtle use of patterns and textures and a lighting system that can capture an array of moods. The result is a serene environment with multiple conversational areas.
Photograph by Daniel Eiffert

MIDDLE LEFT
The mahogany table opens to accommodate large formal gatherings. The simple clean lines of the brushed nickel and frosted glass chandelier play well with the crystal sconces that frame a trio of identical mirrors. Billowy window treatments, diagonally patterned limestone floors and richly colored artwork all work well together.
Photograph by Daniel Eiffert

BOTTOM LEFT
The clients' goal was to create an elegant, minimalist, contemporary apartment that would be a gentle background for their contemporary art. The detail of the recessed panels was used to conceal storage at one end and add interest to the living room wall. Leather-bound sisal-like wool carpeting is the setting for grey textured sofas and aubergine leather chairs.
Photograph by Daniel Eiffert

FACING PAGE TOP
The original master bath was renovated with clean lines. Doors were removed that now open onto the breakfast coffee bar area of the sitting room. The maize-colored terrazzo floor complements the sea-colored glass tile that surrounds the whirlpool bath. A distinctive top-down, bottom-up shade in a textured outdoor fabric maximizes the amount of natural light.
Photograph by Daniel Eiffert

FACING PAGE BOTTOM
The simple, serene feel of this master bedroom was created as part of a complete apartment renovation. The apartment has a sweeping view of the Manhattan skyline. Strategically placed overhead lighting is balanced with task lighting for reading in bed. An Italian-inspired cherry nightstand and custom bed are set against a palette of neutral textures and a white wall.
Photograph by Daniel Eiffert

MORE ABOUT TERE ...

WHAT COLOR BEST DESCRIBES YOU AND WHY?

Red; it is festive and makes me feel like celebrating. I look for any excuse to celebrate with great food and wine and good friends.

WHAT ONE ELEMENT OF STYLE OR PHILOSOPHY HAVE YOU STUCK WITH FOR YEARS THAT STILL WORKS FOR YOU TODAY?

The importance of using good lighting; a room can fall flat if it is not properly lit.

NAME ONE THING MOST PEOPLE DON'T KNOW ABOUT YOU.

I have a spiritual, meditative side that keeps me centered.

WHAT IS THE BEST PART OF BEING A DESIGNER?

The growth that one achieves working with interesting and unique clients.

BERET DESIGN GROUP, INC.
Tere Bresin, ASID
551 Valley Road, Suite 180
Upper Montclair, NJ 07043
New York: 212.223.2898
New Jersey: 973.857.4714
www.beretdesigngroup.com

KAT BURKI

KAT BURKI INTERIORS

It may come as a surprise that an attorney with a business degree segued into a successful career as an interior designer, complete with her own line of home furniture and accessories. But Kat Burki and her intuitive approach to interiors are full of surprises. The self-taught designer began her education in art school, before pursuing law in college, but she never lost sight of her creative passions. Juggling a career as a lawyer with a second vocation as proprietor of a design store, Kat began taking on interior design clients. Soon, it all proved too much. "I took a long vacation and thought hard about what I love to do," she explains. When she returned home, Kat launched the full-service interior design practice she has today. Her creative vision has helped her rapidly rise to success. A contagious passion for design is shared by clients and those who view her warm and sophisticated work.

Kat Burki Interiors is based in Southport, Connecticut, and offers a retail gallery and showroom in addition to full-service interior design. Since its inception in 2002, the firm has completed projects in the greater New York area, including Connecticut and

LEFT
New-meets-old family room: Sophistication and modern amenities create this comfortable yet chic family gathering area with a variety of fabrics, pin-striped moulding and fabric custom designed by Kat Burki.
Photograph by Robert Grant Photography

Rhode Island. Through Kat's nationally marketed product line, the firm's influence can be felt across the country, in the form of upholstered and finely crafted furniture and custom accessories.

Kat is proud of her intuitive approach. "Basically, I need to feel moved; when I get that feeling, I go with my instincts," she explains. She tends to incorporate classic, clean lines and vibrant color schemes that make homes feel at once comfortable and casually elegant. "Each project is about figuring out how to make my clients' lives better and happier," she says, and most clients provide her with full creative license. She enjoys directing the creative vision and showing clients how to reach the goal of a beautiful, functional home.

Her designs have been included in Albert Hadley's "Rooms with a View" and in the Near and Far Aid Designer House Tour, for which she served as the 2007 chairperson. Magazines including At Home, Connecticut Cottages & Gardens, New York Spaces, Panache and Veranda, as well as the book Everyday Kitchens, have covered her work.

Kat also writes a monthly article on design and good taste published in Connecticut's Journal-Register newspapers. With witty, often tongue-in-cheek descriptions, Kat tells readers how to properly hang pictures, use mirrors to open a space or bring more style into their homes. Her approachable, friendly personality and writing have endeared readers and clients alike.

TOP LEFT
City chic meets antique farmhouse. The Scalamadré sofa is adorned by custom pillows and trimming. An Art Deco mirrored coffee table adds interest and allows extra space in a small area. Two antique arched mirrors—taller than the original ceilings—are placed along a wall to bring the outside in and to also add a feeling of space. The mix of florals, oriental prints, stripes and leopard rug all give the room great interest, layering and attitude.
Photograph courtesy of Kat Burki Interiors

BOTTOM LEFT
Breezy Dreams: The mix of woods with white satin and blue and white fabrics creates a heavenly retreat for homeowners to relax and enjoy the views of the garden outside.
Photograph by Robert Grant Photography

FACING PAGE
A beautiful, seamless transition from graceful interiors to the serene waterfront exterior. The moulding has been built out to allow two layers of creamy fabrics to flow, framing the solid French doors. The antique circular table is positioned to provide a place for flowers, books and other objets d' art without blocking the natural scenery. Outside, the wrought iron furniture is cushioned in custom fabrics of beige and blue to once again reflect the serenity of the outdoors.
Photograph by Robert Grant Photography

MORE ABOUT KAT ...

NAME ONE THING MOST PEOPLE DON'T KNOW ABOUT YOU.

My first career was as a lawyer.

HOW WOULD YOUR FRIENDS DESCRIBE YOU?

Mellow.

WHAT IS THE MOST CHALLENGING DESIGN PROJECT YOU'VE UNDERTAKEN?

My own home; I wanted to maintain its 18th-century character while adapting it for today's lifestyle. The project was done in bits and pieces over many years.

WHAT IS THE MOST UNIQUE/IMPRESSIVE/ BEAUTIFUL HOME YOU'VE SEEN AND WHY?

Any of the many early 20th-century homes in Princeton, New Jersey; I love their classic traditional styling and high ceilings.

KAT BURKI INTERIORS
Kat Burki
340 Pequot Avenue
Southport, CT 06890
203.254.2908
www.katburki.com

TIM BUTTON
JOHN STEDILA
STEDILA DESIGN INC.

British artist William Morris said in 1877, "Have nothing in your houses that you do not know to be useful or believe to be beautiful." Tim Button, a principal in New York's Stedila Design, Inc., admits this is advice he would give any homeowner seeking to make a change today. As award-winning designers with more than 30 years of professional experience apiece, Tim and partner John Stedila have designed the interiors of private homes, multi-family residential buildings and retail stores on three continents. Ranked as one of *House Beautiful's* "Top 100 Designers," Stedila Design has a reputation for creativity across a range of styles, and a commitment to environmental responsibility.

"As our business has grown, we have a growing awareness about our responsibility to the community and the environment. We all need to live in a sustainable way that doesn't destroy but rather supports global well-being right here in our own small world," explains Tim. Stedila Design has been involved with several large-scale Green projects,

LEFT
This Central Park West residence's living room possesses an open yet intimate ambience.
Photograph by Scott Frances

59

but applies the same principles and level of consideration to private residences.

The firm worked with Cesar Pelli and Albanese Development on The Solaire, the first Green luxury high-rise residential development in the country to be awarded a LEED (Leadership in Energy & Environmental Design) Gold rating. The Visionaire is another Green condominium project presently in design development. The interiors of both merge the highest standards of environmental responsibility—energy efficiency, healthy and sustainable materials— with beautiful and luxurious designs of the finest quality.

"It is a step-by-step process," describes Tim, adding that the realm of Green design extends beyond finish materials. Stedila Design not only considers whether the carpets and wallcoverings are locally available, recycled or renewable and non-toxic, but they also think about the solvents that will be used to install such finishes.

An attention to detail characterizes all of the firm's work. "No one should come to us for *our* look," explains Tim. "We create a look for who the clients are." As such, their portfolio demonstrates a range of aesthetics, from contemporary to traditional. The staff works closely with clients to create spaces that are glamorous yet understated, current and timeless, and always enriched by the collaboration. "[Stedila Design] has many celebrities and dignitaries as clients, but gives you the same level of service," attests one client in *The Franklin Report.*

Both John and Tim knew from a young age that they wanted to work in design. They each hold degrees from Parsons School of Design. John first gained experience in store design, while Tim worked in product and environmental design. John founded the practice in 1973, and Tim joined him as a partner in 1980.

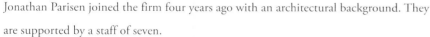

Jonathan Parisen joined the firm four years ago with an architectural background. They are supported by a staff of seven.

The two partners complement one another in skills and practice. Tim describes John as "a brilliant colorist" with an uncanny understanding of color, texture and the relationship of materials. His own strengths are in conceptualizing spatial volumes and how objects relate to an overall composition. While one partner will typically take the lead in a design project, ideas are shared freely and collaboration is frequent. Their plans tend to be consistent in terms of flow and organization, and both partners advocate editing over filling spaces with furniture. "We are a bit minimal even in our traditional work," says Tim.

Stedila Design has been widely published in magazines including *House Beautiful*, *Elle Décor*, *House & Garden*, *Metropolitan Home* and *Metropolis*, and in *The New York Times*. Tim has lectured on environmental awareness in design, and is a member of the

New York Designers Collaborative. John recently completed pro bono design for two facilities for a drug and alcohol rehabilitation facility.

No matter the style or locale of a home Stedila Design has created, all reflect the personality of the homeowner. Tim explains, "People give life to a house, and help make it a welcoming place."

ABOVE LEFT
This historic Southampton beach cottage underwent a complete restoration.
Photograph by Peter Mauss

ABOVE RIGHT
Intricate woodwork and masterful lighting accentuate the voluminous ceilings of the completely restored Southampton beach cottage.
Photograph by Peter Mauss

FACING PAGE LEFT
The bathing area of this Greenwich Village residence features interesting patterns on both the floor and countertop.
Photograph by Richard Mandelkorn

FACING PAGE RIGHT
A fusion of traditional style and modern-day needs, this Greenwich Village bedroom is a delightful place in which to relax.
Photograph by Richard Mandelkorn

MORE ABOUT TIM & JOHN ...

WHAT IS THE HIGHEST COMPLIMENT YOU'VE RECEIVED
PROFESSIONALLY?

That our work is ahead of the curve and that it is current and timeless at the same time.

WHAT ONE ELEMENT OF STYLE OR PHILOSOPHY HAVE YOU STUCK
WITH FOR YEARS THAT STILL WORKS FOR YOU TODAY?

Style never goes out of fashion; and there is an exception to every rule.

IF YOU COULD ELIMINATE ONE DESIGN/ARCHITECTURAL/BUILDING
TECHNIQUE OR STYLE FROM THE WORLD, WHAT WOULD IT BE?

The raised ranch house.

WHAT IS A SINGLE THING YOU WOULD DO TO BRING A DULL HOUSE
TO LIFE?

Take most of the stuff out; leave only what you truly care about.

WHAT BOOK ARE YOU READING RIGHT NOW?

American Gothic: The Biography of Grant Wood's American Masterpiece by
Thomas Hoving.

WHAT IS THE BEST PART OF BEING A DESIGNER?

The clients; when you connect with them and the design gets better for the collaboration.

STEDILA DESIGN, INC.
Tim Button
John Stedila
135 East 55th Street
New York, NY 10022
212.751.4281
www.stediladesign.com

SHERRILL CANET
SHERRILL CANET INTERIORS, LTD.

Expertise in fine antiques, international influences and a classically trained eye are the keys to Sherrill Canet's fresh traditional style. No two projects look the same—each represents the lifestyles and tastes of an individual client— yet all feature a refined balance of old and new. "A common thread in my work is that everything is highly edited," the designer explains. "To be able to mix periods and styles successfully, you have to know when to edit. Too much can be a bad thing." She begins with each project's architecture, using it to inform her choices of furnishings, details and accessories. In projects completed from New York City and Long Island to San Francisco and Palm Beach, Sherrill displays her ability to reduce designs to their essence and complement a home's architecture with beautifully executed interiors.

Sherrill spent her early career as a fashion model, traveling worldwide and living in London, Paris, Milan and Hamburg. She developed interests in photography, design and antiques, and attended London's Inchbald School of Design. Interior design was a natural career path for Sherrill, who combines her varied interests with international sophistication. She also holds a Bachelor of Science degree in economics from Fordham University.

After operating an antiques showroom and providing design consultations on the side, Sherrill transitioned to a full-time interior design practice. Sherrill Canet Interiors, Ltd. has a staff of eight who assist her with designs, including two longtime associates, Christina Danka and Claire Poulikidis. Equally important to the firm as its design proficiency are its project management skills. "Organization is critical to managing multiple large projects at the same time," Sherrill explains.

In addition to her Manhattan office, Sherrill has a satellite office in Locust Valley, Long Island, and plans to open a third location in Palm Beach. Due to debut soon, the Sherrill Canet Home Collection of custom furniture will accompany her already-launched lines of custom carpets available from Stark Carpet and fabrics and wallcoverings from Old World Weavers. The self-described "obsessive" designer is continually redecorating her own home and experimenting with new ideas.

ABOVE
The Sherrill Canet Collection for Stark Carpet featuring Ellipse Design debuted at the 2006 Kips Bay Designer Showhouse.
Photograph by Tim Lee

FACING PAGE
This Gold Coast library features lovely walnut paneling, a red lacquered ceiling and a stunning leather and wool Beauvais floor covering.
Photograph by Tria Giovan

She finds time for philanthropic work with the local Boys Club and hospital, and is involved professionally as an Allied Member of the American Society of Interior Designers, on the Advisory Council of the Robert Allen Showrooms, and as a member of the Locust Valley Chamber of Commerce.

Sherrill's fresh take on traditional has earned praise from national and regional shelter magazines, including coverage in *House & Garden*, *Traditional Home*, *House Beautiful*, *Palm Beach Cottages & Gardens* and *NY Home*. She offers her opinions about design and lifestyle as a contributing editor for *Elements* magazine.

TOP & BOTTOM LEFT
The entire Hamptons beachside retreat is decorated in shades of blue and white, including the kitchen.
Photograph by John M. Hall

FACING PAGE
Fabulous chocolate and silver hand-painted Gracie wallpaper informs this Gold Coast dining room.
Photograph by Tria Giovan

MORE ABOUT SHERRILL ...

WHEN YOU ARE NOT WORKING, HOW DO YOU SPEND YOUR TIME?
Antiquing for work or pleasure or redecorating my own house.

WHAT ONE ELEMENT OF STYLE OR PHILOSOPHY HAVE YOU STUCK WITH FOR YEARS THAT STILL
WORKS FOR YOU TODAY?
Serious editing; too much can be a bad thing.

WHAT IS THE BEST PART OF BEING A DESIGNER?
Trying and doing new things, creating and never being static.

WHAT IS THE MOST UNUSUAL/EXPENSIVE/DIFFICULT DESIGN OR TECHNIQUE YOU'VE USED IN ONE
OF YOUR PROJECTS?
Hand-cut, dried bamboo and metal appliqués were applied on walls to resemble a trellis pattern.

SHERRILL CANET INTERIORS, LTD.
Sherrill Canet
3 East 66th Street, Suite 4B
New York, NY 10021
212.396.1194
www.sherrillcanet.com

JOËL CATURLA
CATURLA DESIGN LLC

Joël Caturla's enthusiasm for design is palpable. His story reads like a portrait of the American Dream: In 1981, he came to the United States from France with aspirations of becoming a successful interior designer. He has achieved his goal through hard work and a passionate commitment to his clients' needs. His European heritage and culture are evident in design projects in Paris, London and New York. After three decades of perseverance, Joël now oversees a staff of four people who are dedicated to servicing his clients. Recognition in top shelter magazines—from *Elle Décor* to *New York Home*—only hints at Joël's achievements.

"I love this country," Joël exudes. "I came here with only my knowledge and a dream—and this is the beauty of America—I have been given the opportunity to succeed." Educated at the École de Pau in the South of France, Joël studied both interior design

and the decorative arts. He then worked and trained under renowned French designer Michel Fortin, becoming an expert in French antiques of the 18th and 19th centuries. When Joël began his own firm, his background taught him to emphasize quality above all else, coining the term "Quality is our Hallmark" to distinguish his practice. Caturla Design aims to create spaces that are contemporary yet universal.

When Joël visualizes and executes a design, every detail is considered. Spatial reorganization, such as repositioning doors and windows or enlarging closet space, is complemented by interior decoration that captures an international elegance no matter the room's period or style. Joël and his team are equally adept at making farmhouse

country appear sophisticated or making urban contemporary appear comfortable. The finest finishing touches, like custom-designed, monogrammed stationery, complete each room.

ABOVE LEFT
Replete with an Ed Bekkerman painting, the grandiloquent main sitting room is a delightful combination of contemporary art, 1930s' accessories and Deco-inspired custom carpet.
Photograph by Peter Margonelli

ABOVE RIGHT
The luxurious bathroom of onyx trimmed with blue marble has a ceramic floor. The 1930s' sconces bring a touch of glamour to the space.
Photograph by Peter Margonelli

FACING PAGE
A serene retreat, the master bedroom boasts golden fabric wall coverings, a recessed ceiling with a shagreen faux finish, ebony Macassar paneling and a sitting area.
Photograph by Peter Margonelli

"I love my business and I work every day with the whole of my heart," Joël explains. His commitment and attention to his clients are clear. In exchange, clients often give him carte blanche to incorporate new and different design ideas. Joël's charm is in not selling his work or himself; instead, he humbly explains that his listening skills are what make his projects successful—and also what have turned many clients into friends. By listening carefully and paying close attention to his clients' needs, he is able to create personalized living spaces. The same ability to work well with others has made Joël a favorite of contractors and craftspeople. He has a great deal of trust in those with whom he works, explaining they are "like a family." This close-knit collaboration between Joël and his select group of painters, upholsterers and cabinetmakers means clients get the utmost quality to go along with the superior service.

Joël does not limit his creative energy to his interior design projects. He has lectured and conducted design tours throughout France. He regularly attends cultural events and art exhibitions to keep his perspective fresh. He also travels frequently throughout Europe. "Everything I see influences me," he explains. An avid reader of histories, Joël is cognizant that understanding the past will keep his present and future designs fresh. With an eclectic blend of work and a story that combines promise and prosperity, Joël's design future is clearly very bright.

MORE ABOUT JOËL ...

WHO HAS HAD THE BIGGEST INFLUENCE ON YOUR CAREER?

French interior designer Michel Fortin, for whom I first worked.

WHAT DO YOU LIKE BEST ABOUT PRACTICING IN YOUR LOCALE?

People in New York City have sophisticated taste and are open to new ideas.

ON WHAT PERSONAL INDULGENCE DO YOU SPEND THE MOST MONEY?

Cultural activities and travel; everything I see influences me, from visiting museums and exhibits to other
artistic pursuits and travel.

HOW WOULD YOUR FRIENDS DESCRIBE YOU?

Ambitious.

CATURLA DESIGN LLC
Joël Caturla
60 West 66th Street
New York, NY 10023
212.799.3250
Fax: 212.721.6261
www.caturladesign.com

ERIC COHLER

ERIC COHLER DESIGN

Eric Cohler contends that he is a regular guy—albeit interior designer, historian, writer, art collector and philanthropist as well. Magazines have dubbed him "the mix-master" for his artful ability to blend elements from different eras with beauty and comfort. Eric is known for encouraging clients to embrace their own personal sense of style. "I'm a khaki pants and blue blazer guy," he admits, equating design to fashion. "I help my clients focus on what is best for them, without being bombarded by what they see in magazines or on television." The honest, straightforward approach yields designs that look timelessly appropriate, and clients who often become friends.

With a master's degree in historic preservation and a certificate in design from the Harvard Graduate School of Design, Eric is known for his architectural approach to interiors. His extensively researched projects meld classic and revivalist design styles with contemporary furnishings and flair. He is fond of scraping away layers of paint to determine original schemes, or finding the right period mantel or furniture to complete a room. He mocks his own curatorial, intellectual process by calling it "house whispering" but says the importance is in learning what a house was or what it has the potential to become.

Eric Cohler Design was established in 1994 and now has 16 employees. Eric sets the design tenor of each project, but delegates responsibilities to his capable team. The firm has completed projects nationally and internationally. Magazines have heralded Eric's stylish and livable interiors and recognized him with *Traditional Home*'s Designer of the Year, *House Beautiful*'s Best of the Best and *International Furnishings & Design Council*'s Designer of the Future awards.

Eric is writing the book *Learning from Lucy*, about 1950s' interior and furniture design as influenced by the "I Love Lucy" television show. He also pens a monthly column in the *American Art Collector*, and writes regularly for the Meredith Publications magazine group. His work has been featured on HGTV, "Find!" and "This Old House," and included in *The New York Times*, *Washington Post* and *Chicago Tribune*.

A self-described "voracious" collector of art, Eric has resorted to keeping pieces tucked under beds and hidden in closets to accommodate his growing collection. The works range from Egyptian sculptures to contemporary paintings, reflecting a survey of art history. Eric aspires to one day leave his artwork to undergraduate alma mater Hobart and William Smith Colleges. His commitment to the schools extends to an internship and travel award Eric sponsors for junior students, underwriting a two-week classical European tour and two-week internship in his office. "I want to empower students," he explains, "If they see the fabric of history, they understand how design can be timeless."

MORE ABOUT ERIC ...

WHAT ONE ELEMENT OF STYLE OR PHILOSOPHY HAVE YOU STUCK WITH FOR YEARS THAT STILL WORKS FOR YOU TODAY?

I tell my clients, "If it works for you, it works for you; don't change what is YOUR style."

WHAT BOOK HAS HAD THE GREATEST IMPACT ON YOU?

There are two: Ayn Rand's *The Fountainhead* and F. Scott Fitzgerald's *This Side of Paradise*.

WHAT IS THE MOST UNIQUE/IMPRESSIVE/BEAUTIFUL HOME YOU'VE SEEN AND WHY?

Mies van der Rohe's Farnsworth House; I love the pure distillation of its form and dissolve between interior and exterior.

WHO HAS HAD THE BIGGEST INFLUENCE ON YOUR CAREER?

My great-grandmother; she visited the 1933 Chicago World's Fair Homes of Tomorrow Exhibition. Particularly struck by architects George and Fred Keck's interpretation, she hired them with one caveat: she wanted the home of *the day after* tomorrow. I've always admired her avant-garde sense of style.

ERIC COHLER DESIGN
Eric Cohler
872 Madison Avenue, Suite 2B
New York, NY 10021
212.737.8600
www.ericcohlerdesign.com

ELISSA CULLMAN

CULLMAN & KRAVIS, INC.

Interior designer Ellie Cullman compares decorating to producing a film. Both require the collaboration of a cast of talents, involve a great deal of editing and refinement and culminate in a public showing. In the early 1980s, Ellie and her friend Hedi Kravis thought the film industry was where they would leave their marks. They drafted a screenplay and showed it to a producer friend. He promptly informed the two that they had "absolutely no talent" as screenwriters but their aptitude for decorating was obvious. He hired them to design his own home, setting their new careers—and the partnership of Cullman & Kravis, Inc.—into motion. Twenty years later, the firm counts four listings on the *Architectural Digest* "AD 100" among an array of commendations.

Cullman & Kravis now has a staff of 20, including senior project managers Jenny Fischbach and Claire Ratliff. After Hedi passed away in 1997, Ellie assumed leadership of the firm. Still passionate about decorating, she remains involved in every project, and is recognized in the industry for her professionalism and creativity. In 2005, Ellie was included on the *Architectural Digest* "Deans of American Design" list of its top 30 visionary designers.

While decorating may have come indirectly as a career path, Ellie always had a love of the arts. A graduate of Barnard College and Columbia University Graduate School, she first worked as an exhibition assistant and curator. Later, she coauthored *Small Folk: A Celebration of Childhood on America* (New York: E.P. Dutton, 1980). Her ability to tell a narrative through artwork is apparent in her interior designs where thematic threads are woven through each project. Designing with fine art and antiques has become such a honed skill that Cullman & Kravis is sought out by collectors.

"Pretty isn't enough," is the mantra by which Ellie and her firm abide. By intentionally layering architectural details, millwork and lighting, decorative elements

ABOVE
The sunroom in Ellie Cullman's own home in Connecticut American boasts faux bamboo and painted furniture, and a striking eagle weathervane that reflects her passion for Americana.
Photograph by Durston Saylor

FACING PAGE
In this sophisticated Manhattan living room, the calm beige palette allows artwork by DeKooning and Southeast Asian sculptures to take center stage. Signature Cullman & Kravis details like the obi-style sash on the chair pillow complete the decoration.
Photograph by Durston Saylor

are enhanced. The detail-oriented designs consider how every element in a room works together. "We always say form and function are the twin pillars of interior design," explains Ellie. "A magnificent space that doesn't function well is a failure." Design schemes range from Park Avenue chic to Connecticut country to Hamptons contemporary.

Cullman & Kravis has always believed in giving back to its community, completing at least one nonprofit decorating job each year. Recent projects have included a medical waiting room at Mount Sinai Hospital and a Brooklyn garden in honor of the late Hedi Kravis. Pro bono work is supplemented by Ellie's own cultural activism, on the boards of the Brooklyn Museum and the Friends of Florence, the Museum of Modern Art's Contemporary Council, and as a past trustee of Barnard College. Recognizing how a love of film helped reveal her passion for decorating, Ellie has been a member of the Film Society of Lincoln Center since 1974.

TOP LEFT
The walls are glazed in "Persian blue," a color which was taken from the ground of the Tabriz carpet, circa 1920. The vibrant Kenneth Noland target painting *Warm Reverie* (1962) is a stunning counterpoint to the arabesques of the rug, and hangs along with 19th-century American masters Martin Johnson Heade and John Frederick Peto.
Photograph by Durston Saylor

BOTTOM LEFT
In a Manhattan study, restrained and elegant materials such as Anigree cabinetry and sleek Ultrasuede walls envelop the owner's art and artifacts, all mementos from his Asian travels.
Photograph by Durston Saylor

FACING PAGE
This crisp modern interior in the Hamptons, designed for collectors of contemporary photography, is muted in palette and minimal in appointments.
Photograph by Durston Saylor

MORE ABOUT ELISSA ...

WHO HAS HAD THE BIGGEST INFLUENCE ON YOUR CAREER?

My late partner, Hedi Kravis, had an incredible innate talent for design; and my Cullman & Kravis colleagues have kept our designs young and fresh over the years.

ON WHAT PERSONAL INDULGENCE DO YOU SPEND THE MOST MONEY?

Flowers; a home isn't alive without fresh flowers.

WHAT DO YOU LIKE BEST ABOUT PRACTICING IN YOUR LOCALE?

New York offers access to an enormous array of talented artisans and craftspeople, from decorative painters to custom metalworkers. New York also has many distinguished antique dealers, and a full schedule of premiere art and antique fairs.

NAME ONE THING THAT MOST PEOPLE DON'T KNOW ABOUT YOU.

I speak fluent Japanese.

CULLMAN & KRAVIS, INC.
Elissa Cullman
790 Madison Avenue, 7th Floor
New York, NY 10021
212.249.3874
www.cullmankravis.com

VANESSA DELEON
VANESSA DELEON ASSOCIATES

One of the fastest-rising stars in interior design today, Vanessa DeLeon is sometimes surprised by her own celebrity. By the age of 28, the designer had already participated on HGTV's "Generation Renovation," "Designer's Challenge," and "Design Star." She has been featured in countless publications including *New York Spaces*, *Design NJ*, *201*, *Latina Magazine*, *Entertainment* and *Time*. Her trademark "Glamilistic" fusion of minimalist décor with glamorous detailing has won clients nationwide. Yet the designer remains grounded; she is committed to a range of philanthropic activities and is quick to point out the inspiration and influence available from one's own family. The youngest designer profiled in *Spectacular Homes of Metro New York*, Vanessa exudes confidence and fresh creativity.

Raised in a family with a proud Cuban heritage and strong creative genes, Vanessa always knew she would have a career in the arts. "I remember looking at my grandparents' photos of Cuba; the architecture was so inspiring," she recalls. Vanessa earned a degree in fashion merchandising from the Fashion Institute of Technology and worked for Ralph Lauren before entering Berkeley College to pursue interior

design. Following the precedent of her family's furniture company, Vanessa started her firm in 2001 to provide both furnishings and complete interior environments.

Vanessa DeLeon Associates is a seven-person firm comprised of individuals with a variety of creative backgrounds, from fine arts to graphics. Vanessa's husband Rolando is responsible for much of the custom furnishings included on projects. The firm maintains a commitment to catering to its clients throughout the design process. It provides a range of comprehensive services so that "having your space designed doesn't become a second job." Vanessa studied feng shui at the Feng Shui Institute of America, and offers this added level of design expertise as requested.

ABOVE
Stainless steel Wolf appliances were added to accentuate the elongated modern stainless pulls.
Photograph by Dan Muro

FACING PAGE
Modern wenge cabinetry and sparkling Silestone countertops add a sleek yet warm feel to this oversized kitchen.
Photograph by Dan Muro

The patented Glamilistic style fuses streamlined furniture and contemporary sophistication with Old World eclecticism. Unusual combinations—a retro lamp with a Louis XV chair—are highlighted in often-monochromatic or neutral color schemes. Sensual materials and luxurious finishes ensure the modern style is never cold. A recent project featured a wall of Italian Bisazza mosaic glass tiles in an intricate quilted pattern.

Before television propelled Vanessa to notoriety, she admits she viewed her youth as a disadvantage. Today, clients seek her out for her creative ideas. "If you want to think outside the box, we'll bring it up a notch," she says. Clients—many of them high-powered stockbrokers and inventors—are often in the same young professional demographic as Vanessa. They can relate to her fresh, innovative perspective.

"I was always taught, 'if you have a little, give a lot,'" says Vanessa. She regularly donates pro bono design services; an example was to a battered women's shelter in southern New Jersey. Vanessa was recently selected as the Honeywell national designer for its classroom makeover donation program. The program provides five teachers each

TOP LEFT
This powder room's wall of glass mosaic tiles adds interest to the modern clean lines of the vanity and the adjacent monochromatic walls.
Photograph by Dan Muro

TOP RIGHT
This master bath was completely gutted to make way for a new sleek and stylish display of clean lines, industrial piping and glamorous silver accents.
Photograph by Dan Muro

FACING PAGE
This elegant, blue-themed dining room got a touch of glamour with its waterfall-inspired beaded chandelier.
Photograph by Dan Muro

year with a $10,000 classroom makeover. "I really like to give back, and wish I could do more," Vanessa adds. She teaches an interior design course at Bergen Community College and is an active member of the American Society of Interior Designers.

In 2007, Vanessa was highlighted as one of *NY Spaces* magazine's "Top 10 Designers Under 40" and won the Ceramic Tile of Italy design competition. Her work has also received several awards from the Interior Design Society, which asked her to be its 2007 guest speaker—following in the footsteps of last year's guest speaker, design legend Holly Hunt.

Vanessa is developing a line of furniture and accessories, and is also working on a potential Web site referencing her trademark style, glamilistic.com. The Web site will be an outlet for Vanessa to fuse her two greatest passions: fashion and interior design. With a promising career in front of her, and the enthusiasm and drive to make herself a household name, Vanessa hopes she might become "the next Martha Stewart."

TOP LEFT
This room was all about the fireplace. It was bumped out, raised to the ceiling and painted with a geometric design to create more visual impact.
Photograph by Dan Muro

BOTTOM LEFT
A striking olive green accent wall gives an unexpected punch of color to the contrast of the dark wenge woods, espresso fabrics and crisp white chairs.
Photograph by Dan Muro

FACING PAGE
This large kitchen is a warm and inviting space thanks to a variety of lighting and tile cut into different sizes to create interest.
Photograph by Dan Muro

MORE ABOUT VANESSA ...

ON WHAT PERSONAL INDULGENCE DO YOU SPEND THE MOST MONEY?

Starbucks, shoes and handbags—you can never have enough!

HOW CAN WE TELL YOU LIVE IN THIS LOCALE?

I am a true city girl; I love the diversity New York City has to offer: a plethora of museums to discover, numerous shopping venues and plenty of diverse restaurants. This only helps to broaden my horizons and expand my creativity.

WHAT IS THE HIGHEST COMPLIMENT YOU'VE RECEIVED PROFESSIONALLY?

I was honored for the "Top 10 Designers Under 40" by *NY Spaces* magazine. It was an amazing accomplishment and compliment to be a part of such a well-established group.

WHAT IS THE MOST UNUSUAL/EXPENSIVE/DIFFICULT DESIGN OR TECHNIQUE YOU'VE USED IN ONE OF YOUR PROJECTS?

A full Bisazza tile wall design for a dining room; these glass tiles are a custom quilted design that costs upwards of $14,000.

VANESSA DELEON ASSOCIATES
Vanessa DeLeon
127 East Ridgewood Avenue, Suite 204
Ridgewood, NJ 07450
201.447.1424
www.vanessadeleon.com

WILLIAM R. EUBANKS

WILLIAM R. EUBANKS INTERIOR DESIGN, INC.

Veteran award-winning interior designer William R. Eubanks has been a presence in New York design for more than two decades, since the company found itself working increasingly on the upper East Coast, with other locations of his interior design business and antiques business in Palm Beach and Memphis. Bill Eubanks is known for his unerring eye for remarkable 17th- and 18th-century antiques, rooms imbued with an unmistakable continental grace and use of rich, textured fabrics and tapestries. Bill and long-time design associate D. Mitchell Brown—now the vice president of design and showrooms—are masters of creating a collector's look. Mitch enjoys putting into practice what he learned long ago at the feet of his mentor, Dallas-based designer Vivian Young: "Put like things together." Gathering different examples of like objects of varying ages into a cohesive group is a way of creating collections for the clients of William R. Eubanks. "We like a room to look timeless, as if it's always been there," Bill says. "We love to have a look that is easy to settle into and looks just as good 20 years from now as the day we installed it."

That does not mean, however, that Bill Eubanks works exclusively on traditionally inspired spaces—most people do not know that in the 1970s, his showroom was highly contemporary. "This is what time has done," quips Bill about the antiques he currently carries and the Old World look that he does so well. "It is a passion and I love it, but I like all aspects of design," he says, "and we still love contemporary design...it's nice to be able to have variety in what we do. All of our clients are individual, and when that front door opens, we should feel the energy of our clients, not William R. Eubanks."

ABOVE
The sylvan view of Central Park from the client's windows inspired the designers to secure a pair of 18th-century paintings from Jacques de La Joue. Louis XV-style antique consoles and a caned chair by Dessin Fournir further complement the setting.
Photograph by Kim Sargent

FACING PAGE
In this entry hall, Bill and Mitch with architect David Hotson increased post-war apartment ceilings from 8 to 10 feet by creating detailed coffers. They also lengthened the central gallery by aligning doorways to give a clean, long perspective.
Photograph by Kim Sargent

The owner of the Manhattan apartment featured here approached William R. Eubanks, Inc. to design a feminine, sophisticated space high aloft Central Park. The firm's design philosophy of creating interiors through collaboration with the client is beautifully illustrated on this project. The client's personal colors and style were influenced by her decision to have the space reviewed by a practitioner of feng shui, who advised the client that certain colors would have beneficial bearing on her spiritual and personal life, including financial and romantic aspects. Bill and his team were already armed with extensive knowledge of the client's preferences and lifestyle, and now with her desire to include new information from the feng shui expert, the designers went to work transforming design concepts into reality. Fortunately, Bill and Mitch were already in Europe on a buying trip for the firm, so they had at their fingertips endless resources from which to select the intense colors the client preferred. For centuries, Europeans have lived by candlelight, so Europe is a treasure trove of fabrics of bright, sun-drenched colors. Voila! Bill and Mitch returned to the States to show the client fabric selections to fulfill her every requirement. The client is delighted with the finished product, because the design incorporates both the personality of the client and the recommendations of the feng shui practitioner. Bill and Mitch describe the apartment as a feminine, sophisticated space that adheres to the principles of feng shui—exactly as the client wants.

With a worldwide reach when it comes to projects, the firm excels in taking exceptional care of those clients, too. William R. Eubanks has a 3,500-square-foot, sunlit showroom in the heart of Palm Beach, along with a separate design center, which boasts a full-service staff of designers, project coordinators and architectural personnel, as well as an extensive library of fabric, finishes and floor coverings. All design services are orchestrated by Bill and Mitch. Not only is Mitch involved on both the design side and styling the showrooms, he also works with Bill on antique-buying trips in Europe, where they scour the countryside for the best finds at the best prices.

The antiques side of William R. Eubanks is a thriving business in its own right. Bill remembers sage advice he received from fellow antiquarian and friend Kenneth Neame, a London-based designer, who urged him to have an antiques business alongside his interior design business. "Once you develop a passion for antiques, it's like gambling," says Bill, who enjoys searching for unique pieces across England, Italy, Spain, Portugal

and France, just to name a few places. He is always looking for new and different ideas, as travel is a critical, constant education for designers. Since falling in love with the English countryside years ago, Bill continues to be a regular visitor and has been profoundly influenced by the way the English live with gorgeous objects from all eras.

ABOVE LEFT
No stone has been left unturned. Every space, including the terrace, has been thoughtfully designed—there is a place for breakfast, another to visit and a niche for reading. Gregorius Pineo iron furniture completes the composition.
Photograph by Kim Sargent

ABOVE RIGHT
A stone Quatrain table extends the living room outside to the terrace, which overlooks Central Park.
Photograph by Kim Sargent

FACING PAGE
Silk velvets, damasks, stripes, chinoiserie motifs, tapestries and trims from Lelievre, Stark and Clarence House—a few of the designers' favorite things—inform this stunning setting.
Photograph by Kim Sargent

Regardless of the destination, however, Bill believes that the more we travel, the more we pursue, and says, "Travel takes us to worlds we would never go otherwise." With numerous different projects ongoing at any given time, he is deeply satisfied in the quest for fantastic finds. An added benefit to Bill's procurement travels is the broad exposure he has to different cultures and their respective color palettes, forms, ideals and ways of life. His clientele is comprised of well-traveled professionals and aesthetes who often desire to be surrounded by things that inspire them, things they have seen or experienced in their own travels. In the rare instance that the designer has not personally experienced the requested style or cultural flavor, he gladly arranges to visit the source of inspiration to ensure that he can exceed patrons' expectations.

Every day brings something new, and to Bill that is the beauty of the design business. At the end of the day, it is the connection with the client that truly matters. When one client finally saw her apartment on New York's Fifth Avenue, she declared that she had never been so happy. "She said 'You've been inside my head,' " recalls Bill. "When a client feels that way, we know we've been successful with what we do. My greatest happiness is experiencing the joy of a pleased client at the end of a project."

RIGHT
The striking interior accents direct attention outward to this spectacular view. Rock crystal obelisks, 19th-century Canton vases as lamps, a pair of 18th-century landscapes by Frans Swagers and bronze doré gueridons set an elegant tone.
Photograph by Kim Sargent

This joy is achieved through a philosophy of Billy Baldwin that the entire William R. Eubanks team has taken to heart—knowing the client first. Though in eras past, some designers had the luxury of being able to live literally with clients to glean an intimate understanding of their needs and stylistic preferences prior to designing for them, today's busy lifestyles simply do not afford that depth of research. Bill and Mitch, however, make a point of getting to know their clients just the same. By visiting clients at their places of residence, they are able to pick up on cues that may not come to light in ordinary conversation. They seek to understand every facet of their clients' lives—how they eat, sleep, entertain, relax, travel and more. Acting as "spatial psychologists," they observe the sum of decorative objects the client has selected over the years and look for common themes that may elucidate the person's true tastes, which can then be translated into fresh new interiors. Bill and Mitch's ultimate goal is to bring forward their clients' finest tastes; devoting their lives to this mission and achieving thoughtful designs on a daily basis has resulted in a host of lifelong friends who have truly spectacular homes.

MORE ABOUT WILLIAM ...

WHAT IS THE BEST PART OF BEING AN INTERIOR DESIGNER?

While I'm driven to create beautiful interiors and love finding gorgeous objects, the aspect of my work I prize most is sharing time with my clients, who, as a group, have an almost unlimited array of life experiences—they often become close friends.

DESCRIBE YOUR STYLE OR DESIGN PREFERENCES.

I have a preference for 17th- and 18th-century continental and English design, but I enjoy working in all periods.

WHAT COLOR BEST DESCRIBES YOU AND WHY?

Red. It gives vitality and zing to one's surroundings, and it makes any space more exciting. Every room needs a touch of red.

Photograph by Kim Sargent

William R. Eubanks and the vice president of design and showrooms, Mitch Brown.

WILLIAM R. EUBANKS INTERIOR DESIGN, INC.
William R. Eubanks, Allied Member ASID, Associate Member
IIDA, Professional Member ICA/CA
David Mitchell Brown
400 East 59th Street, Suite 5F
New York, NY 10022
212.753.1842
www.williamreubanks.com

400 Hibiscus Avenue
Palm Beach, FL 33480
561.805.9335

174 Collins Street, Suite 101
Memphis, TN 38112
901.452.6975

BARCLAY FRYERY

BARCLAY FRYERY

"My weakness is that I do what I will and get what I want." Although the statement was uttered by Oscar Wilde more than a century ago, it could have been said by Barclay Fryery just last week. The celebrated interior designer, lifestyle expert, event planner, newspaper columnist and television personality lives life according to the principles of Indulgence, and encourages his clients to do the same. "I don't mean that coarse, glutton-esque, bottomless-basket-of-breadsticks kind of indulgence. I mean the art of creating a more satisfying life," Barclay declares. With his trademark wit and tell-it-like-it-is attitude, Barclay encourages his clients to live, learn and evolve every day. He will focus his design expertise on everything from clothing to home décor by examining who his clients are and who they can be. "I never elevate people beyond their personal range, or what is appropriate for their region, architecture and climate," he promises.

Indulge: Seven Ways to a Fabulous Life (or wardrobe, career or home, for that matter) is the title of Barclay's soon-to-debut book series. It is all about living life without "strauma" (stress and drama). He recognizes that people are often too busy to establish a personal style. The well-traveled designer wants his clients to slow down, take a vacation and get out of their comfort zones. Seeing and appreciating new things will uncover likes and dislikes that could never be found by flipping through magazines. "Never think that you have to follow anyone's rules. Rules in decoration are boring and are meant to be broken."

Born Timothy Mark Barclay Fryery in Meridian, Mississippi, the designer grew up appreciating his mother's clean, personal style—even if was from the Sears Roebuck catalog. His first commissions were decorating the dorm rooms of college mates at Ole Miss. He launched his professional career more than 25 years ago in Greenwich, Connecticut, and has completed projects and worked with clients around the world. Listed on *House Beautiful*'s "Top 125" list a half-dozen times, Barclay has also been featured in *Elle Décor*, *Marie Claire* and *Maison Francaise*.

ABOVE
This living space features an exquisite blend of contemporary and traditional.
Photograph by Chi Chi Ubina

FACING PAGE
The soft colors and elegant symmetry of this bedroom enhance its warmth.
Photograph by Chi Chi Ubina

His weekly "Ask Barclay" column in the *Greenwich Post* propelled him to popularity, and winning USA Networks' "House Wars" designer challenge in 2003 sealed the deal. Barclay's design advice has been featured on TV shows including E!'s "Style Court," the "CBS Early Show" and ABC's "Good Morning America." His line of couture furnishings will soon be marketed in multiple countries, and he recently inked a deal for a six-episode television program with Dr. Phil. Barclay also is exploring opportunities to market a line of home furnishings at Target stores.

For many, the name Barclay Fryery is already synonymous with living life to the fullest, in beauty, comfort and, most of all, happiness. There is no doubt that once his philosophy hits the mainstream, he will be helping many more people realize that style is not such a secret after all.

TOP LEFT
Natural light infuses this kitchen and nicely plays up the clean palette of white cabinetry, richly stained wood floors and stainless steel appliances.
Photograph by Chi Chi Ubina

BOTTOM LEFT
The chic design of this outdoor entertaining space can even be enjoyed from within the home.
Photograph by Chi Chi Ubina

FACING PAGE LEFT
A modern painting sets the tone for this living area.
Photograph by Chi Chi Ubina

FACING PAGE RIGHT
Rich hues and bold wall art—juxtaposed with a flower arrangement atop the nightstand—create a dramatic effect in this bedroom.
Photograph by Chi Chi Ubina

MORE ABOUT BARCLAY...

WHAT ONE ELEMENT OF STYLE OR PHILOSOPHY HAVE YOU STUCK WITH FOR YEARS THAT STILL WORKS FOR YOU TODAY?

Live, learn and evolve every day. Find the best of the best and share it with the world. In short, Indulge.

WHAT IS THE BEST PART OF BEING AN INTERIOR DESIGNER?

Giving my clients what they never, ever thought they wanted but absolutely love.

WHO HAS HAD THE BIGGEST INFLUENCE ON YOUR CAREER?

My mother; she has exceptional personal style.

WHAT WOULD YOUR FRIEND DESCRIBE YOU AS?

A gentleman.

BARCLAY FRYERY
Barclay Fryery
Greenwich – Paris – Vienna – Los Angeles – South Beach
271 Greenwich Avenue
Greenwich, CT 06830
www.askbarclay.com

103

ALEXANDER FURMAN
TRACEY FURMAN

SALISBURY & MANUS INTERIORS

Parents of three children under the age of six, Alexander and Tracey Furman have carved an interior design niche by creating comfortable, livable and traditionally beautiful homes for young families. Designing primarily in the English classical aesthetic, the partners promote sophisticated color schemes, the use of patterns and elegant formality, advocating "we're all about comfort." Together with partner Michael Sullivan and a staff of nine full-time employees, they are Salisbury & Manus Interiors. In conjunction with its Upper East Side showroom, the firm provides custom interior design services to clients throughout the country.

Alexander, a graduate of Union College, is the third generation in the interior design business. Tracey studied fine art at Marymount University and in Florence, Italy. Michael's design training came from the fine arts program at the Rhode Island School of Design. When they formed the partnership more than a decade ago, the goal was to cater to clients who wanted to create beautiful homes but lacked the time to do it themselves. They understand and appreciate the pace of modern family life, and design beautiful spaces that accommodate this lifestyle. "We have

an understanding of what people want today," Alexander explains. "We're a young family in Manhattan with small children; we can relate to our clients' needs."

The other priority for the firm has always been to ensure quality service and high-end products. Salisbury & Manus employs its own tradespeople, who are able to provide decorative painting, upholstery, millwork and furniture fabrication on a highly customized and faster schedule than traditional outsourcing. Tracey, Alexander and Michael oversee every project from inception to installation, insisting on their own craftspeople to ensure guaranteed delivery and exceptional quality. The firm also operates an extensive e-commerce Web site where clients can purchase a singular item or outfit an entire house with fine decorative furnishings from around the world.

ABOVE
The resident of this Long Island home chose a hand-painted hunting scene mural for his dining room that incorporates images of his family members.
Photograph by Tim Lee

FACING PAGE
The use of over-scale comfortable upholstery was chosen for the living room of this sprawling Hamptons oceanfront home.
Photograph by Tim Lee

Salisbury & Manus' approach is hands-on not only with its craftspeople but also with its clients. Highly collaborative, the partners and staff work with their clients to create homes in a range of styles, from formal French to English country, emphasizing classical proportions, balance and symmetry. Contrary to the muted earth tones popular today, they recommend the use of bold colors such as red, yellow and green. They encourage homes that feel as alive and energetic as the families who reside within.

LYNN GARELICK
LBG INTERIOR DESIGN

When Lynn Garelick recounts her path to interior design, it is filled with the unexpected and colored by life experiences—not unlike her interiors. After spending her childhood in Hawaii, where she was influenced by the natural colors and beauty of the islands, Lynn moved to San Francisco. She pursued her passions for art and history at the University of California at Berkeley, and obtained a graduate degree in education, to allow her to share these passions with others. Lynn subsequently lived around the country—from Minneapolis and Denver to Detroit and New York—following her husband's career and raising two sons. She continued to draw and paint in her free time, never losing sight of her artistic interests.

Lynn's frequent relocations—and new houses to decorate—brought out an interest in decorating. As friends and neighbors regularly asked for advice, and her children began to grow up, Lynn was determined not to become a housewife who decorated, but a real designer. She worked part time for a series of firms and earned a Certificate in Interior Design from the New York School of Interior Design, always balancing her career aspirations with maintaining a household and caring for her family. Once

her children had grown, Lynn worked full-time for Anne Mullin Interiors, refining her design skills and learning to service high-end clientele. In 2001, she founded her sole proprietorship, LBG Interior Design.

Thirty years of professional experience has taught Lynn well how to create attractive homes by working closely with her clients. "The relationship has to be there before design can begin," she says. The collaborative designer is known for her teamwork with clients, describing her role of refining and executing each client's vision.

Lynn brings beauty and comfort to the colors and styles that each client prefers, working in a range of traditional and contemporary aesthetics. "Good taste is always the bottom line," she advocates. With careful editing so that interiors never look overdone, Lynn creates a sense of luxury that people notice from the moment they walk into a room. Quality and casual elegance are emphasized within environments that feel at once comfortable and impressive.

In addition to maintaining her practice, Lynn is involved with numerous philanthropic efforts at her church. She recently completed an in-depth project to develop a history of the 350-year-old Christ Episcopal Church in Greenwich, which will become a key tool in a multi-million-dollar capital campaign. Also active professionally, Lynn is an NCIDQ-licensed designer and a full professional member of the American Society of Interior Designers. Ever committed to her family, Lynn still finds time for regular visits with her grown children and grandchildren.

TOP LEFT
One is invited into the comfortable upstairs sitting area at the Greenwich Designer Showhouse—2007, Greenwich, Connecticut. The chair and ottoman are custom designed by Lynn Garelick, the antique secretary is English, circa 1800. The antique painting *A View of the Brittany Coast* is by American Prosper Senat. The "Thistle" light fixture is courtesy of Niermann Weeks.
Photograph by David R. Sloan

BOTTOM LEFT
The hallway in the upstairs sitting area at the Greenwich Designer Showhouse is enhanced by a woven and patterned wall covering from Brunschwig & Fils. The antique English Regency card tables provide a base for whimsical wire sculptures by Rodger Stevens. Monotype prints *Brooklyn One and Two* by Mary Manning, an antique French dressing mirror and a custom designed bench complete this interesting area.
Photograph by David R. Sloan

FACING PAGE LEFT
A Han Dynasty horse, Tang Dynasty censers and a Bodhisativa bust rest on an antique Chinese altar table, circa 1810, in the East Sun Room at the Merrywood Designer Showhouse.
Photograph by David R. Sloan

FACING PAGE RIGHT
A quiet corner in the East Sun Room contains a McQuire open armchair, custom sofa, antique fabric pillows and a Carole Gratele coffee table. The Phillip Jeffries "Paperweave" wall covering is enhanced by Chinese antique carved window panels.
Photograph by David R. Sloan

MORE ABOUT LYNN ...

WHAT IS THE BEST PART OF BEING A DESIGNER?

Always having a new project; each one is different and is a fresh creative challenge.

WHAT ONE ELEMENT OF STYLE OR PHILOSOPHY HAVE YOU STUCK WITH FOR YEARS THAT STILL WORKS FOR YOU TODAY?

I have always created comfortable, casually elegant interiors.

WHAT IS A SINGLE THING YOU WOULD DO TO BRING A DULL HOUSE TO LIFE?

Develop a master color scheme that flows from room to room, creating an interesting flow of related colors throughout the house.

WHAT DO YOU LIKE ABOUT PRACTICING IN YOUR LOCALE?

I work in an attractive area on Long Island Sound, where the scenery is always changing. The people here have diverse backgrounds and are willing to try new approaches. Their adventuresome attitude makes my job a lot of fun.

LBG INTERIOR DESIGN
Lynn Garelick, ASID
172 Field Point Road, #7
Greenwich, CT 06830
203.625.8375
www.lbginteriordesign.com

KATHI GERNAT
KATHI GERNAT INTERIOR DESIGN

"No challenge is insurmountable," says Kathi Gernat. With her trademark upbeat attitude and can-do practicality, Kathi has made a name for herself as a talented and creative designer who has fun with the process. She brings her clients along for the enjoyable ride. "Interior design shouldn't be like going for a root canal," she says with a laugh. In any array of styles, Kathi's designs feature comfortable elegance personalized for each client. "When my clients tell me they love coming home, that's when I know I've done my job," she says.

By asking a lot of questions and—most importantly—listening to her clients' answers, Kathi is able to elicit true feelings about design. "People often don't know what they want," she explains. "I draw them out." From strong and bold concepts to soft and monochromatic schemes, the range of Kathi's interior designs demonstrates her flexibility satisfying any client's whim. She says the biggest misconception people have about the design process is that they will not have input. "Clients are afraid it won't be 'their' house." Kathi explains that she asks a lot of questions to decorate houses that are ideal for each client—not for herself. The aesthetic choices are always client-driven, so that at the end of the day, their house is one they will be proud to call home.

Many of Kathi's projects begin during the very early stages of new construction or renovation. She works regularly with architects to coordinate interior design that is integral to a home's architecture. She has collaborated with a longstanding team of installers, painters, upholsterers and other specialty craftspeople with whom she works closely to execute quality projects. Her ability to work so well with others ensures cohesive results.

ABOVE & FACING PAGE
In this marvelous contemporary living room in Rye, New York, the artwork speaks through design. The extensive Southwest art and sculpture collection took precedence—it shines through, unobstructed by the design.
Photographs by David R. Sloane

Kathi originally studied art history as an undergraduate. After marriage and family, she longed to get back into an artistic career. Helping friends with decorating challenges always piqued her interest, and Kathi thought it would be a good idea to pursue this creativity. She expanded on her education by taking a variety of design courses and has operated her own interior design practice since 1987. Maintaining her own practice has always allowed her to balance family—her first priority—with her career.

Kathi has completed projects in the New York metropolitan area and along the East Coast, from Florida to Maine. She has also decorated houses in Arizona and Colorado. "It is fun to be able to incorporate different looks from all parts of the country," she explains. Kathi is inspired by vernacular design, and also by designers whose work she reads about. The voracious reader is particularly impressed by the work of

John Fowler and Mark Hampton as well as contemporary designers. Kathi divides her time between Connecticut and New York; in addition to being close to clients in both locations, the arrangement affords the designer plenty of opportunities to visit museums and the theater, two of her favorite pastimes.

Along with operating her practice, Kathi has taught interior design at Fairfield University for the past several years. In a seminar-style course called "The Business of Interior Design," she and other professionals describe the practical side of operating a successful design business. "Design is often a long, arduous process," she tells her students. "But the finished product is uplifting—and always worth it."

MORE ABOUT KATHI ...

ON WHAT PERSONAL INDULGENCE DO
YOU SPEND THE MOST MONEY?

Travel; I just returned from Venice—a magnificent city.

WHAT COLOR BEST DESCRIBES YOU
AND WHY?

Yellow; it is happy.

WHAT BOOK ARE YOU READING
RIGHT NOW?

Paris: The Biography of a City by Colin Jones.

IF YOU COULD ELIMINATE ONE DESIGN/
ARCHITECTURAL/BUILDING TECHNIQUE OR
STYLE FROM THE WORLD, WHAT WOULD
IT BE?

Faux Palladian windows; they are rarely appropriate
for a home's architecture and they pose many interior
design issues.

WHAT ONE ELEMENT OF STYLE OR
PHILOSOPHY HAVE YOU STUCK WITH FOR
YEARS THAT STILL WORKS FOR
YOU TODAY?

Have fun along the way.

WHAT IS THE BEST PART OF BEING
A DESIGNER?

Seeing beautiful things every day.

KATHI GERNAT INTERIOR DESIGN
Kathi Gernat, Allied Member ASID

225 East 79th Street
New York, NY 10075

2 Soundview Drive
Greenwich, CT 06830
203.622.1310
www.kathigernatinteriordesign.com

GLENN GISSLER

GLENN GISSLER DESIGN, INC.

Interior designer Glenn Gissler will tell you that the two elements you need to enliven a home are artwork and friends. "Design is about incorporating a sense of warmth and humanity," Glenn explains. His award-winning, 10-person firm, Glenn Gissler Design, Inc., is known for creating elegantly understated environments that are as functional as they are handsome. With a degree in architecture and lifelong interests in 20th-century art, literature, fashion, historic preservation and architectural history, Glenn brings to the design process design work that is stylistically diverse, but beautifully crafted and integrated into the architecture of the space.

Glenn has a refined pragmatism that is first and foremost at the service of those who will inhabit the homes he creates. It is more important for him to enhance the lives and reflect the values of his clients than it is to utilize a single decorative style. While his work is defined by earthy sophistication, his projects draw upon aspects from both classicism and modernism and often incorporate antiques as key sculptural elements. Glenn's affinity for old objects—even within modern contexts—stems from his keen knowledge of, and interest in, art and architectural history. He

coyly explains that he likes to "add a little B.C." to every project. The results are an engaging interpretation of the client's personality and life or work style, inspiring a sense of greater self-expression and personal satisfaction.

His role in larger residential projects is expansive and includes assisting clients in the selection of architects, contractors, lighting specialists, landscape designers and other consultants. Once the team has been established, Glenn's involvement includes working on the schematic design of the architecture of the project, site visits during construction and aesthetic evaluations for design intent incorporating both architectural and interior design elements.

Multiple collaborations with repeat clients attest to Glenn's skills in both design and client satisfaction. He has maintained ongoing relationships with his clients, including a highly profiled fashion designer for whom he designed numerous projects. For a client in the financial sector, Glenn has designed a large duplex apartment in New York City as well as the family's residences in Westchester and Martha's Vineyard. Glenn equates interior design to portraiture, comparing the differences in artistic style and medium to the different homes a person might occupy. "Each house reinterprets the values of people who live there."

Glenn has had a long-term commitment to interior design and architecture. He knew he wanted to be an interior designer as early as 13 years old, and with the encouragement of a number of inspired teachers, he cultivated his unique creative spirit. A native of Milwaukee, Wisconsin, Glenn was active in historic preservation.

He attended the Rhode Island School of Design, earning dual degrees in fine arts and architecture. In 1987, shortly after moving to New York City, he founded Glenn Gissler Design, Inc. with a primary focus on residential projects in the New York metropolitan area, and has established a diverse portfolio that includes residences in Westchester, Long Island, New Jersey and Florida.

ABOVE LEFT
Understated custom oak paneling provides a rich backdrop for art works by Jacques Lipchitz, Franz Kline and Roy Lichtenstein with a sculpture by Diego Giacometti adding a lighthearted accent in the library of an art collector.
Photograph © William Abranowicz / Art + Commerce

ABOVE RIGHT
A French bronze chandelier from the 1940s hangs over a table designed to complement the Jules Leleu chairs. A painting by Ross Bleckner provides striking visual drama for this sophisticated dining room.
Photograph © William Abranowicz / Art + Commerce

FACING PAGE
A bronze sculpture, art books sitting on a mahogany center table and a gilded Regency stool are framed by the dark stained wood for the floors and doorway to create a dramatic and inviting entry into the living room.
Photograph © William Abranowicz / Art + Commerce

He remains active in areas that hold his passion—he is a member of the National Trust for Historic Preservation, the American Society of Interior Designers and the Designers Collaborative. Glenn lives in Greenwich Village in Manhattan with his wife Susan Harris, a talented contemporary art critic and curator, and their young daughter.

Glenn's work has received wide acclaim because of his ability to craft timeless yet unique designs as well as his impeccable attention to details. He has been included in *House Beautiful* and *New York Magazine*'s "100 Top Designers" lists and as one of 50 "Insiders of American Design" in *Elements of Living*. His work has been featured in *The New York Times, Elle Décor, House & Garden, House Beautiful, Town & Country, Interior Design, Hamptons Cottages & Gardens, Shelter Interiors* and published in many books.

TOP LEFT
The muted palette of the master bedroom in this Greenwich Village apartment creates a sense of calm and serenity. Works on paper by Louise Bourgeois and Alan Saret are paired with an antique Chinese bronze vase used as a lamp that sits on an antique wood table with curvaceous legs.
Photograph by Gross and Daley

BOTTOM LEFT
A vintage Dunbar table holds an eclectic selection of decorative arts and books. Drawings from the 1960s by Nancy Spero, and from the 1990s by Leon Golub, hang over a luxuriously deep sofa in a rich earthy green fabric.
Photograph by Gross and Daley

FACING PAGE
A pair of French chairs from the 1930s, an antique Thebes stool and other decorative objects are combined with art and books in this living room to create a warm and sophisticated environment.
Photograph by Gross and Daley

MORE ABOUT GLENN ...

FROM WHERE DO YOU DRAW INSPIRATION?

Inspiration for me starts with my clients—how they currently live, and more importantly, their hopes, wishes and desires for the future.

WHO HAS HAD THE BIGGEST INFLUENCE ON YOUR CAREER?

My third grade art and painting teacher; she and other teachers taught me there aren't any boundaries to creativity.

WHAT IS THE HIGHEST COMPLIMENT YOU'VE RECEIVED PROFESSIONALLY?

My best awards have been inclusion on a variety of "best of" lists—*New York Magazine*, *Elements of Living*, *House Beautiful* and *New York Home*. I like feeling included with my respected peers.

GLENN GISSLER DESIGN, INC.
Glenn Gissler
36 East 22nd Street, 8th Floor
New York, NY 10010
212.228.9880
www.glenngisslerdesign.com

SUSAN ZISES GREEN

SUSAN ZISES GREEN, INC.

Not many internationally recognized designers are forthcoming enough to reveal a major project disaster. But Susan Zises Green, thrice listed on House Beautiful's "Top 100 Designers" roster, is known as much for her warm and giving personality as she is for her timeless, sophisticated interiors. On her very first project, and eager to display her organizational skills and openness as well as her creativity, Susan presented her client with a detailed list of every item to be included in his redecorated home, complete with sources and prices. He promptly dismissed the decorator and did the project himself. Since beginning her career in 1968, Susan has not forgotten the lesson.

She balances beauty with practicality, advocating livable, comfortable houses that express clients' personal styles. "People want to really live in their homes, rather than have off-limits spaces. Whether formal or informal, comfort and luxury can always be the underlying elements." She believes successful decorating projects go hand-in-hand with client intimacy. By developing strong client relationships, Susan is able to create spaces that surround clients with things they love, evoke their sense of whimsy, and capture the essence of their family.

Susan's decision to study interior design came about when she witnessed designer David Barrett decorating her parent's home. He encouraged her to enroll in the New York School of Interior Design. When Susan graduated, she turned down the opportunity to work for Barrett—although honored by his offer—and opened her own practice instead. In nearly four decades, creating dream homes has been the firm's mainstay, completing projects up and down the East Coast. Susan has participated in the coveted Kips Bay Decorator Show House seven times and has been published in magazines ranging from *Architectural Digest* and *Town & Country* to *Cosmopolitan* and *Connecticut Cottages & Gardens*. *The Washington Post* and *The New York Times* have covered her work, and the television show "Find!" visited her Connecticut country house.

ABOVE
This intimate recessed seating area for quiet conversation or reading is in a rather grand living room. The view overlooks the beautiful planted terrace off of this room.
Photograph by Durston Saylor

FACING PAGE
Anchored by slatted, cream-color shutter doors and khaki-toned, interestingly patterned fabrics, the Kips Bay Decorator Show House room is an informal space filled with natural ease, elegance and modernity. Trowel marks add texture to the hand-painted vanilla walls with custom-mixed mica flecks. Atop sisal carpet, the unconventional seating arrangement suits a modern lifestyle—a space to eat, lounge and work.
Photograph by Billy Cunningham

"My father raised his kids to always help other people," Susan explains. "We learned at a young age the importance of giving back." The lesson has guided her extensive charity work, including establishment of a foundation, Americans—We Are a Family. She is also active in the Women's Campaign Forum, a nonpartisan organization that supports women's political advancement.

Susan looks for inspiration in everyday items, from the fresh flowers she adorns her home with weekly to her many collections, including outsider art, antique majolica and vintage textiles. Texture, color and pattern may be inspired by the past, but the resulting designs capture the very real design challenges of present-day life. Susan's only signature is that all of her work is exceptionally well done. "Houses, like people, are always changing and I so enjoy the process."

TOP LEFT
In his private "writing room" the owner of this apartment can read, write and relax, perhaps with a visitor or two.
Photograph by Durston Saylor

BOTTOM LEFT
The butterscotch-color walls create an inviting and warm environment in a large living room with an intimate seating area facing the fireplace.
Photograph by Susan Zises Green

FACING PAGE
A long view from the dining room through the entry hall to the living room reveals a gracious and well-lived-in apartment.
Photograph by Michael Moran

MORE ABOUT SUSAN ...

WHAT IS THE MOST UNIQUE/IMPRESSIVE/BEAUTIFUL HOME YOU'VE SEEN AND WHY?

I am a huge fan of old Nantucket architecture. The history and integrity of the designs are incredible. I admire the pioneers in the 1600s and 1700s and their clean, simple, yet entirely gracious and functional aesthetic.

WHAT IS THE HIGHEST COMPLIMENT YOU'VE RECEIVED PROFESSIONALLY?

The loyalty of my clients; one of my favorite clients is a family that I have worked with for more than 20 years in several cities. They have proven to not only be loyal clients but also very important friends.

WHEN YOU ARE NOT DESIGNING, WHAT CAN YOU BE FOUND DOING?

Entertaining, always. I love designing parties and see entertaining as an adjunct of design; it is all about sharing what you have and enjoying life with others.

ON WHAT PERSONAL INDULGENCE DO YOU SPEND THE MOST MONEY?

My weekly flower budget; I adore flowers and creating interesting arrangements throughout my home.

SUSAN ZISES GREEN, INC.
Susan Zises Green, ASID
475 Fifth Avenue, 12th Floor
New York, NY 10017
212.824.1170
www.susanzisesgreen.com

Jay M. Haverson
HAVERSON ARCHITECTURE AND DESIGN

For architect Jay Haverson, the design process is all about meeting—and exceeding—his clients' expectations.

"It is a listening and translation process," as he describes his firm's highly personalized approach, adding that all his clients come with good ideas. His approach is to translate their ideas into something unexpectedly creative. This element of surprise lends freshness and drama to the work of Haverson Architecture and Design. Incorporating contrasts and color, including features such as unique architectural elements and sequences or specialty lighting to highlight spaces, are all ways the firm adds a little something extra. Regardless of project budget or size, Jay promises, all clients get at least one element that is special or new.

Founded in 1983, Haverson Architecture and Design has an impressive and diverse portfolio of residential, commercial and restaurant projects across the country and around the globe. Rather than advocate a singular style, the firm promotes its more generalist approach—a unique décor for every project based on contemporary, transitional and traditional design. For residential design, whether the style is Craftsman, Shingle, Neo-Classical or Contemporary, Jay and his staff are committed to exquisite detailing and incorporating the needs and desires of the clients.

Jay earned a Master of Architecture from Columbia University and a Bachelor of Architecture cum laude from Syracuse University. He is a registered architect in 17 states, a member of the American Institute of Architects and formerly sat on the Town of Greenwich Historic District Commission.

Jay credits his wife and partner, Carolyn, with keeping him and the entire firm grounded. "She is the person everyone goes to for advice or knowledge; she's a terrific critic," he describes. Trained as a graphic designer, Carolyn is responsible for signage and identity design for much of the firm's commercial work.

ABOVE
Entry hall at the Trump International Tower Apartment, New York, New York.
Photograph by Paul Warchol Photography

FACING PAGE
A room with a view from the 32nd floor, New York.
Photograph by Paul Warchol Photography

Additionally, her primary role is as business manager, overseeing firm operations. "She's our touchstone," Jay says, describing his wife's balance of being both artistic and practical at the same time.

The Haversons are joined by two partners, 18 architects and two interior designers. With nearly all staff members trained as architects, the firm brings a distinctly architectural perspective to its work. The way spaces are organized, colors and materials are selected and lighting is incorporated refers to core architectural principles and reinforces cohesiveness. "Our interior designs and decorative elements always enhance the architecture," Jay explains.

Projects by the award-winning firm have been featured in *The New York Times*, *Interior Design*, *Architectural Record*, *Architecture Magazine*, *New York Magazine*, *This Old House*, *Home*, *Greenwich Magazine*, *The Greenwich Time*, *New York Spaces*, *New York Magazine*, *GQ* and *Dream Homes New England*.

MORE ABOUT JAY ...

WHAT ONE ELEMENT OF STYLE OR
PHILOSOPHY HAVE YOU STUCK WITH FOR
YEARS THAT STILL WORKS FOR
YOU TODAY?

Stand by the basic principles of design, plus a twist or
two, to equal design success.

WHAT IS A SINGLE THING YOU WOULD DO
TO BRING A DULL HOUSE TO LIFE?

Paint it to match the personality of the clients.

WHO HAS HAD THE BIGGEST INFLUENCE
ON YOUR CAREER?

My father; although he died when I was very young,
he saw the desire in me to be creative and encouraged
me to become an architect. He continues to inspire me
every day.

WHEN YOU ARE NOT WORKING, WHAT
CAN WE FIND YOU DOING?

Walking our dogs with my wife (and partner)
Carolyn—rain or shine!

HAVERSON ARCHITECTURE AND DESIGN
Jay M. Haverson, AIA
63 Church Street
Greenwich, CT 06830
203.629.8300
www.haversonarchitecture.com

DARREN HENAULT

DARREN HENAULT INTERIORS, INC.

Standing in the doorway of a room designed by Darren Henault might offer an elegant view, but it will not give you the full impression. The subtle sensuality of Darren's designs invites you to enter, sit down and get comfortable. Listening to the rustle of silk taffeta drapes at an open window or appreciating a chair's intricate upholstery pattern are part of the experiential design Darren Henault Interiors, Inc. aims to achieve with every project. Design schemes capture the individuality of every client, through an eclectic blend of traditional styling infused with personal effects—seeming at once cosmopolitan and comfortable.

Comfort is more than a design philosophy for Darren. His quick sense of humor and easygoing manner make those who know him at once comfortable as well. He cites children's book character Curious George with influencing his curiosity about life, vows never to wear white after Labor Day and admits to a collection of extravagant fur hats. Through his tongue-in-cheek musings, one thing is clear: Life's experiences are most important. As such, in his designs, the experience is paramount. Every detail is considered, and every piece of furniture, artwork and finish material is chosen for its effect as part of the overall composition, and as it will be enjoyed up

close in everyday life. And just as Darren's strong personality is clear, he ensures the personalities and lifestyles of his clients are duly reflected in their homes.

Darren's ability to capture feelings comes from his own exposure. His father's textile company taught him about color, texture and craftsmanship. After graduating from Boston University, he worked briefly in advertising before enrolling in FIT's interior design program. He started his design career creating custom upholstered furniture before beginning his decorating practice in 1995. Frequent travel to Japan, India, Egypt, South America and Europe has offered him cultural context. "I credit my travels with heavily influencing my design sensibilities," Darren explains. He is able to bring the feelings instilled in him in different places to his work. "My goal isn't to

ABOVE
A "faux" skylight was added to bring light into a long hallway. The custom mouldings were finished with automobile paint for added luster.
Photograph by Mark Lohman

FACING PAGE
A TriBeCa loft bedroom features a custom mahogany bed and nightstands. A cashmere headboard and throw offer luxury while hand-painted walls lend visible texture.
Photograph by Tim Bell, www.timothybell.com

design spaces that only look good in photographs," he avows, but instead to create spaces that require full immersion to appreciate the layers of thoughtful detail.

Darren is modest about his work, which has been widely published in such magazines as *Vanity Fair*, *Elle Décor* and *House & Garden*. "Design is a passion; it is a feeling that is hard to quantify," he describes. He brings this passion to decorating projects across the country, and to volunteer work on the board of the Callen-Lorde Community Health Center.

MORE ABOUT DARREN ...

WHAT IS THE MOST UNIQUE/IMPRESSIVE/BEAUTIFUL BUILDING
YOU'VE SEEN AND WHY?

The Frick Museum in New York; the solidity of the design makes it feel like such a
safe place.

WHAT DO YOU LIKE BEST ABOUT PRACTICING IN YOUR LOCALE?

In New York, I get to work on city apartments, beach houses, country homes, cabins, ski
chalets—all this in one state.

WHAT COLOR BEST DESCRIBES YOU AND WHY?

It's not possible to limit myself to one—but anything on the Farrow & Ball color chart.

WHAT ELEMENT OF STYLE OR PHILOSOPHY HAVE YOU STUCK WITH
FOR YEARS THAT STILL WORKS FOR YOU TODAY?

Be timeless, not trendy . . . and never wear white after Labor Day.

DARREN HENAULT INTERIORS, INC.
Darren Henault
180 Varick Street, Suite 424
New York, NY 10014
212.677.5699
www.darrenhenault.com

Barbara Hillier

RMJM HILLIER

A ward-winning international architecture, urban planning and interior design firm RMJM Hillier is best known for its large-scale projects such as academic campuses and pharmaceutical headquarters. With more than 300 design professionals, the firm is a recognized and well-respected market leader for major commissions. Its recent merger with RMJM has created one of the most geographically and culturally diverse design practices worldwide. Each year, RMJM Hillier takes on a select few private residential projects, demonstrating its equal proficiency for detail-oriented domestic scale work. Principal Barbara Hillier, AIA, oversees many of these residences, explaining the firm's philosophy, that "each project must be the unique expression of the client's dream," is just as applicable.

LEFT
Here, rooms are defined by spatial cues. The entertainment area is defined spatially through the millwork and area rug; the dining room, by artwork.
Photograph by Paul Warchol

Houses are an opportunity for RMJM Hillier's designers to get involved with every detail, shaping spaces through light, color, custom millwork and custom furniture. "It is an alchemy of personalities," explains Barbara, comparing the design process to musical composition. She takes her design cues from a home's existing architecture and from a collaborative relationship with clients, generating spaces that are unpredictable and expressive.

"We like to import clients' experiences into their spaces," says Barbara. She spends a large amount of time getting to know her clients, often taking them to showrooms to identify natural affinities for colors, textures, forms and aesthetic styles. By talking with the clients of the Manhattan apartment pictured here, Barbara learned of their extensive travels and collection of Japanese art. This, in combination with an understanding of the apartment's

architecture—and its spectacular views of Central Park and the East River—influenced the open floor plan with sliding walls. The design allows for maximum views and daylight, but affords privacy when needed. Exploring historic themes in Japanese architecture influenced the material choices and the sliding wall design reminiscent of shoji screens. The renovated apartment offers display potential for the artwork in a clean environment that suits the clients' lifestyle and entertaining needs.

Barbara has more than 25 years of professional experience. She earned undergraduate degrees from Temple and Arcadia Universities and also studied at the University of Pennsylvania. A registered architect, she is a member of the American Institute of Architects, Society for Environmental Graphic Designers and the National Trust for Historic Preservation. She has lectured and written extensively about design. She

writes, "Architecture is experienced as the artful blend of objective reason and subjective impression that can elevate the human spirit in the process of meeting its desired expectations for habitation and performance. Regardless of size or purpose, each project is a puzzle waiting to be solved. It is through listening to the client and respecting the physical surroundings that sets the range of possibilities."

ABOVE LEFT
The hideaway kitchen and morning room beyond are revealed through a sliding screen.
Photograph by Jeff Tryon

ABOVE MIDDLE
In the dressing area, 28 feet of wardrobe are nicely concealed within flush wood paneling leading to the teak-wrapped bath.
Photograph by Paul Warchol

ABOVE RIGHT
The serenity of the home's Asian-inspired design extends into one of three bathrooms.
Photograph by Jeff Tryon

FACING PAGE
Space is made flexible via the use of sliding screens, allowing spaces to connect or remain separate.
Photograph by Paul Warchol

MORE ABOUT BARBARA ...

WHAT IS THE BEST PART OF BEING A DESIGNER?

Appreciating all we have; seeing, absorbing and not taking things for granted.

WHAT DO YOU LIKE ABOUT PRACTICING IN YOUR LOCALE?

New York is the world of fashion and glamour; if there is something new to be seen, it is there to see.

WHAT IS THE HIGHEST COMPLIMENT YOU'VE RECEIVED PROFESSIONALLY?

I really appreciate when clients say the design process has been fun.

WHAT SINGLE THING WOULD YOU ADD TO BRING A DULL HOUSE TO LIFE?

Color; it livens any space.

RMJM HILLIER
Barbara Hillier, AIA
275 Seventh Avenue, 24th Floor
New York, NY 10001
212.629.4100

500 Alexander Park
Princeton, NJ 08543
609.452.8888
www.rmjmhillier.com

Noel Jeffrey

THE JEFFREY DESIGN GROUP

Striking a balance between comfort and style, Noel Jeffrey designs interiors and furnishings that are classically timeless and always inviting. "Your home should be a showplace, but it should also be cozy," he advocates. His 12-person firm, The Jeffrey Design Group, has been in business for nearly four decades, providing interior design and decorating with a full complement of additional creative services, including architectural design, art and antique acquisition and even special event design. Noel retains creative oversight on all projects, helping to ensure that his characteristic creative vision is integrated fully among the design teams and into every project.

Quality and eclecticism are two of the hallmarks of Noel's work. "Our projects may be seen as truly individualized expressions of a client's tastes and wants, rather than being bound by a set style," states the firm's interior design philosophy. Juxtaposing furnishings from the 18th through the 20th centuries in a single interior offers the element of surprise. Using only the finest furniture or artwork of any era lends a classical sophistication. The ultimate goal is always a space that appears timeless, not trendy. While Noel's use of color has been called "daring," it is more about

careful combinations than audacity. He advises pairing bright or shocking tones with neutrals, adding that balance and control are extremely important. "Generally speaking, I tell my clients to be bold, not timid," he states.

House & Garden magazine wrote that Noel "has an enviable gift for finding the perfect object." Extensive travel, innumerable resources and refined taste ensure he will find what is most appropriate. And when he cannot identify the perfect piece, Noel will create one. His custom furniture designs range from upholstered pieces to cabinetry—even a grand piano.

Noel received a Bachelor of Fine Arts from Pratt Institute, and studied at Columbia University's School of Architecture. Soon after founding The Jeffrey Design Group in 1969, the firm established its well-regarded reputation. The dapper Noel, known for impeccable taste and design ingenuity, is something of a media darling. He has been published in all of the major shelter magazines, including *Architectural Digest*, *Avenue*, *House Beautiful*, *House & Garden*, *Interior Design*, *Robb Report* and *Metropolitan Home*. The author of two books on design, *Interior Design: The Designer's Style* and *Design Diary: Innovative Interiors*, Noel has also appeared on HGTV, PBS and CNN. His work has been featured in more than a dozen books on decorating and interior design. His elegantly inventive and widely appealing work is found in New York and its suburbs, California and Florida.

MORE ABOUT NOEL ...

WHEN YOU ARE NOT DESIGNING, WHERE CAN YOU BE FOUND?

In the country, I spend time in my garden. In the city, I enjoy theater, reading and taking walks.

WHAT IS THE BEST PART OF BEING A DESIGNER?

The creative part; it only amounts to about 15 percent of the work—you spend the other 85 percent translating the creative concept into reality.

WHAT IS THE HIGHEST COMPLIMENT YOU'VE RECEIVED PROFESSIONALLY?

I'm happy when my clients are happy; compliments are lovely, but the client's reaction is what matters.

WHAT IS THE MOST BEAUTIFUL BUILDING YOU'VE SEEN?

The Palace of Versailles.

THE JEFFREY DESIGN GROUP
Noel Jeffrey
215 East 58th Street
New York, NY 10022
212.935.7775
www.noeljeffrey.com

MAGDALENA KECK
MAGDALENA KECK INTERIOR DESIGN

Combining balanced comfort and subtle stimulation of the senses within contemporary interiors has been the design approach for the design studio Magdalena Keck Interior Design, which was established in 2001. Magdalena Keck relies on her artistic background and patient, detail-oriented approach to help clients create homes that reflect their personalities and lifestyles. Her goal is to create spaces that "look and feel effortless and do not look staged." She achieves this through careful layering of objects from different time periods and origins. Pieces are selected or designed with great care. Only what is needed and beautiful—nothing else—finds its place in the designer's interiors.

Magdalena grew up and attended college in Poland, where she studied fine arts and painting. A visit to New York just prior to graduation inspired a new career direction in interior design. She soon relocated to the city and enrolled in the interior design program at the Fashion Institute of Technology. She worked her way through school, so that by the time she graduated, she had the knowledge and experience to establish

LEFT
A 1960s' Brazilian rosewood and cane table is paired with Edward Wormley dining chairs from the same era.
Photograph by Jonathan Keck

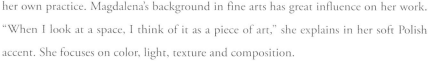

her own practice. Magdalena's background in fine arts has great influence on her work. "When I look at a space, I think of it as a piece of art," she explains in her soft Polish accent. She focuses on color, light, texture and composition.

Magdalena believes in keeping clients involved in the design process. Her collaborative, hands-on approach means she spends many hours talking and shopping with clients, and often becomes close with them. In doing so, Magdalena's residential interiors display individuality as well as refinement.

In addition to residential designs, Magdalena also creates interiors for restaurants and retail spaces. Her full-service capabilities extend beyond traditional design and decorating to include identity development, environmental graphics, visual merchandising and custom furniture and fixtures. Creating everything from the décor to the menus ensures consistency. "I like going between residential and commercial design," says Magdalena, explaining that while residential design is very emotional and intuitive—learning and incorporating each client's personal preferences and habits—commercial design involves more utilitarian elements.

Magdalena was commissioned to renovate a Frank Lloyd Wright-designed house in Westchester, New York. "I adore the fact that the structural materials are the decorative ones—brick, wood, concrete and glass—and materials on the outside of the house are the same as on the interior." One of Magdalena's recommendations for all homeowners is to simplify. "Probably throw away 75 percent of things," she half-jokes. Un-cluttering interiors is a sure way to make spaces appear clean and genuine. Magdalena's streamlined designs have been published in *Interior Design*, *VM+SD* and *Kitchen and Bath Design News*.

ABOVE LEFT
The side table is adjacent to integrated white lacquer bookshelves.
Photograph by Jonathan Keck

ABOVE RIGHT
The dark glossy Edward Wormley night table complements the softness of the wool and linen custom bed and luxurious silk rug.
Photograph by Jonathan Keck

FACING PAGE TOP
A Miró print is the focal point of the living room. Small-scale, yet comfortable furniture is accented with the Grasshopper lamp by Greta Magnusson Grossman.
Photograph by Jonathan Keck

FACING PAGE BOTTOM
Stainless steel contrasts custom walnut cabinets and the end-grain butcher block. Wax and oil finishing brings out the natural character of the wood.
Photograph by Jonathan Keck

MORE ABOUT
MAGDALENA ...

WHAT COLOR BEST DESCRIBES YOU
AND WHY?

Gray; it is understated, yet powerful, and can
have unexpected effects.

WHAT ONE ELEMENT OF STYLE OR
PHILOSOPHY HAVE YOU STUCK WITH
FOR YEARS THAT STILL WORKS FOR
YOU TODAY?

Less is more; you don't need a lot to create a space
that feels right, just the right amount of color,
texture, form and light.

WHO HAS HAD THE BIGGEST
INFLUENCE ON YOUR CAREER?

My clients; they inspire and challenge me.

WHEN YOU ARE NOT DESIGNING,
WHERE CAN YOU BE FOUND?

Hiking in the Catskills or
Adirondack Mountains.

MAGDALENA KECK INTERIOR DESIGN
Magdalena Keck
12 West 27th Street, 10th Floor
New York, NY 10001
212.725.7704
www.magdalenakeck.com

ROBIN KEY

ROBIN KEY LANDSCAPE DESIGN

A good interior designer will often speak of clean lines, quality materials, comfortable spaces and inspiring views. Robin Key will describe the same qualities in her own work. However, she is not an interior designer. Instead, she is a landscape architect recognized for creating outdoor rooms with the same attention to detail and varied design aesthetics as one who practices indoors. Her landscape architecture firm, Robin Key Landscape Design, completes projects ranging from small urban rooftop and backyard gardens to expansive country estate gardens. Sensitive to client needs, community contexts and the environment as a whole, Robin Key Landscape Design approaches its work with a collaborative spirit and award-winning creativity.

The firm seeks design solutions that respond to both the surrounding architecture and site conditions. A contemporary house might be complemented by a limited plant palette with specimen trees. An expansive property might have a layered arrangement of large and small trees, shrubs and perennials. Robin's strength is her knowledge of plant material and her ability to effectively organize outdoor spaces. Working extensively in the urban environment, she has broad experience with

shade-loving perennials and shrubs. "We like to use as much native plant material as possible," she explains. This makes the landscape much more maintainable. Creative problem-solving—such as combating voracious deer appetites or identifying plants that grow in sandy beach soil—is a critical part of successful designs.

The firm's landscapes reflect each client's style and wishes. "I like to design gardens so clients actually use them," explains Robin, who spends a lot of time talking with clients about how they will use outdoor spaces alone and in conjunction with indoor rooms. She is mindful of views out from indoors, and how garden furniture relates to furnishings inside a home. She often specifies outdoor furniture to encourage flexibility. Ottomans that multi-purpose as tables or seating are a popular inclusion. The firm works closely with craftsmen who share a commitment to quality materials and workmanship.

In two decades of practice, Robin's firm has become known for its hands-on approach and close client relationships. She earned a bachelor's degree in plant and soil science from the University of Vermont and completed graduate coursework in landscape architecture at Cornell University. The licensed landscape architect practiced for 10 years before beginning her own firm in 1987. Today she is joined by two associates; the team accepts a limited number of projects each year to ensure a high level of attention to each one.

A native of Ireland, senior associate Gareth Mahon studied engineering in Dublin and Glasgow, Scotland, before moving to the United States to pursue a career in landscape design. He received his Masters of Urban Design degree at City College New York where he performed graduate research in sustainable design in Ecuador.

His interest in urban spaces led to his design taking first place in the Williamsburg Waterfront Design Competition for the East River in Brooklyn.

Associate Erin Moriarty holds a Master of Landscape Architecture degree from Cornell University and a Bachelor of Science in Ethnobotany from Vassar College. She has a vast knowledge of plants, landscape elements and cultural traditions from around the world and has taught courses on environmental responsibility to both children and adults.

In addition to practice, Robin donates services to several schools and churches. At her weekend home in Vermont, Robin has extensive woodland, perennial, vegetable and fruit gardens and participates in the Vermont Tree Farm Program. The firm has volunteered for Habitat for Humanity's Bronx Row House Project. This combination of design and hands-on involvement lends balance and perspective to every member of the team.

Robin Key Landscape Design has been recognized with the Greenwich Village Society for Historic Preservation's Front Stoop Award in both 2006 and 2001.

MORE ABOUT ROBIN ...

WHEN YOU ARE NOT WORKING, WHERE CAN WE FIND YOU?

Working in my Vermont garden weeding, moving plants around, experimenting. I also love to cook the wonderful food that my husband produces in our vegetable garden.

WHAT IS THE BEST PART OF BEING A DESIGNER?

Collaborating with others on design ideas, problem-solving and having the opportunity to research and explore different materials, plants and construction methods.

WHO HAS HAD THE BIGGEST INFLUENCE ON YOUR CAREER?

The landscape architect Jens Jensen.

WHAT IS A SINGLE THING YOU WOULD DO TO BRING A DULL HOUSE TO LIFE?

Develop beautiful views to enjoy while looking out from the inside.

ROBIN KEY LANDSCAPE DESIGN
Robin Key
333 Hudson Street, Suite 1001
New York, NY 10013
212.229.2534
www.rk-ld.com

PHILIP LA BOSSIERE

LA BOSSIERE ASSOCIATES, INC.

Interior designer Philip La Bossiere asserts, "I am not a beige guy in any sense of the word" in reference to both his colorful interiors and his exuberant personality. He has spent the past 20-plus years cultivating his reputation as a sincere, hands-on decorator with timeless and unexpected design schemes. Always excited by Continental furniture, either at auction or abroad, Philip prefers strong contrasts, rich color schemes and a dash of the exotic. He was educated at Parsons School of Design, and in apprenticeship to renowned designer David Barrett, where he learned to execute designs that are timeless without ever feeling conservative.

Philip's overriding design philosophy is to keep things in context, explaining "there's a fine line between the unexpected and what is out of place." He understands the importance of working within the given conditions, from each client's individual personality and preferences to the budget and characteristics of the physical space. After all, he says, "you can't turn a contemporary house into an English pub."

He loves textured walls, and often uses raffia or upholstered fabric to bring depth and softness to a space. "In order for a room to be comfortable, it has to look comfortable," Philip believes. He is partial to dark colors and monochromatic compositions. Custom furniture designs often make their way into his spaces. Strong working relationships with tradespeople ensure Philip's design vision is crafted with the utmost level of attention to details and quality.

Since opening his practice in 1987, Philip enjoys repeat and referral business. He has been rehired by members of a single family for six different projects. The value he places on relationships, coupled with his ability to interpret the emotional lifestyle of each client, means he often engages in other creative pursuits for his patrons. He has been known to help with party planning and event design, and even decorates one family's Christmas tree each year.

La Bossiere Associates, Inc. is a boutique design practice; its size allows Philip to be personally involved in each project, maintaining the close relationships that have contributed to his success. He is assisted by a close-knit team, outsourcing specialists as necessary. Projects have been featured in *The New York Times*, *New York Spaces*, *New York Newsday*, *New Jersey Monthly*, *The Bergen Record*, *Hampton Style*, and *201 Magazine*. Philip has also received praise for his participation in the Hampton Designer Showhouse, the Junior League of Montclair Showhouse, the Designer Showhouse of New Jersey and Mansions in May, the Designer Showhouse of Morristown.

TOP LEFT
The entry foyer's stone floor and architectural-block wallpaper create a warm backdrop for a collection of exotic antiques.
Photograph by Peter Rymwid, www.PeterRymwid.com

BOTTOM LEFT
Walls stenciled with a Gothic trellis in tones of mango set a tropical pace for the solarium.
Photograph by Peter Rymwid, www.PeterRymwid.com

BOTTOM RIGHT
In the corner of this large white living room, comfortable club chairs are positioned amidst valued collections.
Photograph by Peter Rymwid, www.PeterRymwid.com

FACING PAGE
18th-century street maps of Paris envelop the kitchen. Antique French lanterns over the island add to the Old World atmosphere.
Photograph by Peter Rymwid, www.PeterRymwid.com

MORE ABOUT PHILIP ...

WHAT BOOK HAS HAD THE GREATEST IMPACT ON YOU?

In The Pink: America's Most Fabulous Decorator by Carleton Varney. She brought drama and excitement to every room she touched!

WHAT IS THE MOST UNUSUAL/EXPENSIVE/ DIFFICULT DESIGN OR TECHNIQUE YOU'VE USED IN ONE OF YOUR PROJECTS?

I designed the complete interior of a 1950s' vintage wooden yacht. The challenge was to maximize design efficiency within the small spaces without compromising comfort, luxury or function.

WHAT IS A SINGLE THING YOU WOULD DO TO BRING A DULL HOUSE TO LIFE?

Add color; the right shade gives a room instant personality.

WHAT ONE ELEMENT OF STYLE OR PHILOSOPHY HAVE YOU STUCK WITH FOR YEARS THAT STILL WORKS FOR YOU TODAY?

Keep things in context—client's personality, physical space, budget and color combinations.

LA BOSSIERE ASSOCIATES, INC.
Philip La Bossiere
154 West Saddle River Road
Saddle River, NJ 07458
201.825.7123

KRIS LAJESKIE

KRIS LAJESKIE DESIGN GROUP

In 2006, Kris Lajeskie came to New York to create a residence for long-term patron clients. Kris transformed the penthouse of Charles Gwathmey's boutique building at Astor Place into a rich and elegant interpretation of her dramatic, yet understated, artisan-influenced style. "The project was so inspiring and successful," she recalls, "I made the commitment to expand my firm and set up shop in New York."

Returning to New York brings Kris full-circle. Born and raised in New Jersey, she worked in retail management for 12 years for Macy's West in Los Angeles and San Francisco. Seeking solace and self-discovery after her corporate career, she moved to Santa Fe, New Mexico, in the mid 1990s. There, her innate design talents were cultivated as she embarked on a four-year project called Rancho Alegre.

The 26,000-square-foot adobe compound is set on 200 acres, reminiscent of a Spanish Colonial village. It was Kris' first foray into design, but an all-encompassing one. Extensive research into museum archives and history books as well as conversations with

the area natives helped her recreate architectural details, interiors and furnishings with authenticity and accuracy. Involvement with master artisans revived several "lost art" techniques intrinsic to Western, Native American and Spanish-Mexican cultures. The unique high desert project became a beacon for Kris' design skills and projected her into the realm of clients seeking the same vision of artisan- and authenticity-driven creations.

"Bringing an international vision, an organic sensibility and the signature mark of master artisan collaboration to every creation" is the mission by which Kris and her studio abide. She has since expanded from Santa Fe to Milan and New York. Spending nearly a third of every year in Europe—particularly Italy—offers Kris the opportunity to develop new design resources and cultivate relationships with artists around the world. "Frequent trips to Europe have exposed me to the juxtaposition between old and new, classical and contemporary, craftsmanship and innovation," she describes.

Kris' design vision continues to evolve with a line of custom furniture. She is particularly passionate about her collaboration with Italian lighting designer Enzo Catellani. For five years, she has been cultivating a United States market, importing and distributing the hand-made lighting for clients, projects and design professionals. She has also been featured on two HGTV programs.

Kris' trademark interiors are completely custom to the client and space. Her process is both spontaneous and dynamic, invigorated by the heart and soul she puts into every project. She articulates her work as "a fine balance between understanding the expectations of the client and their lifestyle and respect for the architecture and region." Ever inspired by nature and master artisans, Kris infuses her unique vision to create original and authentic interiors in New York and around the world.

TOP LEFT
A still life composition in perfect balance, the room boasts a custom-designed table and commissioned stainless drape. Sculpture by Magdalena Abakanowicz, Gebert Contemporary.
Photograph by Francis Dzikowski/Esto

BOTTOM LEFT
Smoke and amethyst tones create a calm respite for the master bedroom. Venetian-plaster textured walls serve as a dramatic backdrop.
Photograph by Francis Dzikowski/Esto

FACING PAGE
Warm earth tones and luxurious textures enhance the media room/library's relaxing and comfortable environment.
Photograph by Francis Dzikowski/Esto

MORE ABOUT KRIS ...

WHAT IS THE BEST PART OF BEING AN INTERIOR DESIGNER?

My life and work are one. Everywhere I go, there is always a place, an object or a person that informs my work. I also feel very fortunate to have this vision to see and feel a complete creation in my mind's eye before the pen ever touches the paper.

WHAT DO YOU LIKE ABOUT PRACTICING IN NEW YORK?

The city is an incredibly dynamic environment—full of great clients, great talent and spectacular architecture to work with. Best of all, it's exactly the center point between Santa Fe and Italy!

WHAT IS THE MOST UNUSUAL/EXPENSIVE/DIFFICULT DESIGN OR TECHNIQUE YOU'VE USED IN ONE OF YOUR PROJECTS?

I commissioned a Parisian artist to weave stainless steel wire draperies. We made history by collaborating with the famed Aubusson weavers in France, using looms that have woven tapestries for royalty since the 15th century.

KRIS LAJESKIE DESIGN GROUP
Kris Lajeskie, ASID Industry Partner
Santa Fe – New York – Milan
The Caledonia
450 West 17th Street, Suite 1606
New York, NY 10011
646.510.2882
www.krislajeskiedesign.com

RONA LANDMAN

RONA LANDMAN, INC. INTERIOR DESIGN

Balance has always been an important component of Rona Landman's work and life. In her interior designs, she strikes a balance between timeless forms and elegant functionality. In practice, she equalizes outstanding design with superior customer service, believing follow-through is one of the most important aspects of her job. Professionally, Rona has balanced her sole proprietorship practice, Rona Landman, Inc. Interior Design, and related professional activities, with her personal dedication to raising two children. And, she has done it all while still finding time to hone her championship golf game on the weekends.

Rona has been featured in *Architectural Digest*, *New York Spaces*, *New York Newsday* and *Manhattan Style*, for her mid-century-inspired interiors. Her designs draw extensively from forms of the 1940s and beyond, in combinations that are both complex and soothing. "I am a neutralist at heart," Rona explains. Her interiors typically incorporate soothing color palettes of neutral shades. Bursts of color, elements of texture and works of art lend visual excitement to keep the eye engaged without overwhelming. "Restraint is so important," she adds. The effect is always

to create for the homeowners a tranquil environment that seamlessly merges form and function.

"My clients' homes should be an extension of their personalities," believes Rona, who uses her best sense of style and professional knowledge to create results that exceed expectations. She takes pride in her honest, straightforward approach and her detail-oriented practice. Floor plans and elevations are always drawn meticulously, and craftspeople and contractors are carefully supervised so that interior designs are executed flawlessly. Although she is the vision behind her firm's work, Rona has two assistants and a draftsperson to ensure client service and design success are maintained throughout all phases of a project.

ABOVE
Glossy chocolate wallpaper from Stark provides a backdrop for *Kissing in Tropics*, from the series in chocolate by Vic Muniz.
Photograph by Peter Rymwid

FACING PAGE
Aptly dubbed "Sweet Dreams," this American Hospital of Paris 2005 Showcase Home room features Cindy Sherman's 1983 painting, *Swimmer*.
Photograph by Peter Rymwid

After earning a Bachelor of Fine Arts in Commercial Art from Long Island University, Rona initially pursued a career in graphic art. Realizing that was not the right choice for her, she went back to school—this time to the New York School of Interior Design—and earned a second degree. She founded her namesake firm in 1995 following more than a decade in practice with others. Today, the firm is based in a studio apartment in the Upper East Side of Manhattan, and manages projects throughout the New York, New Jersey and Connecticut region.

In addition to practicing, Rona is an advocate of breast cancer awareness. She supports the "Pink Tournament" golf fundraising tourney. An avid golfer herself, Rona has won four championships. She has participated in a variety of showcase homes for charitable organizations, including the American Hospital of Paris Foundation and the Southampton Hospital Foundation.

MORE ABOUT RONA ...

NAME ONE THING MOST PEOPLE DON'T KNOW ABOUT YOU.

I have a fear of heights; I can't even stand on an apartment balcony.

IF YOU COULD ELIMINATE ONE DESIGN/ARCHITECTURAL/BUILDING TECHNIQUE OR STYLE FROM THE WORLD, WHAT WOULD IT BE?

Santa Fe Style.

WHAT IS THE MOST UNIQUE/IMPRESSIVE/BEAUTIFUL HOME YOU'VE SEEN AND WHY?

Taliesin West, Frank Lloyd Wright's winter home in Arizona; I love the way it lets the outside in.

WHAT DO YOU LIKE BEST ABOUT PRACTICING IN YOUR LOCALE?

The subway; getting around is easy and convenient in New York.

RONA LANDMAN, INC. INTERIOR DESIGN
Rona Landman
185 East 85th Street, Suite 20A
New York, NY 10028
212.996.8171
www.ronalandmaninteriordesign.com

BARBARA LANE

BARBARA LANE INTERIOR DESIGN

Interior designer Barbara Lane offers abundant advice on how to make a home feel livable and comfortable. Personalizing a house with artwork or photography, accenting rooms with texture or color and mixing styles are all ways she has brought elegance and chic eclecticism to her clients' homes. "It's safe to live your life in neutrals, but one needs a little zip every now and then just to keep it interesting," she believes. Whether that zip comes in the form of a splash of color or a French antique, Barbara ensures it will capture the personality of the homeowner.

Barbara's signature style begins with a contemporary look that is warm and inviting. Soft edges and abundant natural light work in tandem to convey feelings of comfort. Barbara often employs unexpected materials—parchment, mica, straw, embossed leather—to lend a rich texture and depth to surfaces. She consults a team of specialized craftspeople, many of them European, to incorporate techniques and expertise not typically seen in the United States, such as for elaborate, illuminated cabinetry. She brightens rooms with sheer fiber window panels that let in diffused natural light. The effect is always for clean lines and subtle detailing, often to enhance clients' extensive collections of art or antiques.

A collector of pop art from the 1950s and 1960s and mid-century Italian art, Barbara loves to incorporate her clients' art collections into designs. She has done so with items ranging from paintings to Chinese antiques, and has also acquired pieces and commissioned in situ works on behalf of clients. These special acquisitions from contemporary artists may someday become "the antiques of the future."

Barbara also has an interest in all things French, maintaining an apartment in Paris so that she can regularly visit on sourcing trips. She buys the little touches—antique lamps, small side tables and mirrors—that she says "give a house its soul." She keeps these special purchases in storage to be used as foils or as complements alongside her own custom furniture designs or contemporary pieces.

Barbara credits her education with her careful attention to how rooms flow into one another. Her effective space planning is enhanced by working closely with architects on most projects. Barbara's decorating concepts extend to interior architectural modifications, such as enlarging doorways in both width and height to enhance connectivity between rooms.

Barbara first studied English, earning a Bachelor of Arts, Phi Beta Kappa, from New York University. She went to work as a teacher on the west side of Chicago, but soon changed career directions to interiors. She enrolled at the Harrington Institute of Design at Illinois Institute of Technology. Upon graduation with a certificate in interior design, she practiced professionally from 1973 until 1985, also pursuing graduate coursework at Pratt Institute.

TOP LEFT
A Parisian guest bedroom in cool neutrals pairs soft textures with the romance of a Vik Muniz photograph and the graphic simplicity of Matisse.
Photograph by Thierry Malty

BOTTOM LEFT
A Hamptons master bedroom features silk linen carpeting for a luxurious feel mixed with horsehair end tables and antique Mategot nesting tables.
Photograph by Thierry Malty

FACING PAGE
Parchment walls line a master bedroom in Paris as a backdrop for French antiques by Chareau and Mategot, and custom silk rugs. The open door provides a view of the wood-paneled master bath beyond.
Photograph by Thierry Malty

From 1985 until 2003, Barbara put her interior design career on hold to run a variety of museum projects. She was head of the patron's group and served on the board of the Guggenheim Museum in New York. As president of the American Friends of the Israel Museum, Barbara was heavily involved with the Jerusalem museum's endowment campaign. However, when a friend asked for decorating help in 2003, Barbara was lured back into the profession. "I had given away my drafting equipment years earlier," she remembers with a laugh, adding that computers had become the norm in the interim, so it did not matter. The enjoyable project quickly resurfaced Barbara's creativity and design skills.

Barbara Lane Interior Design was reestablished in 2003, and provides design services in the greater New York area, including the Hamptons and Connecticut as well as in Florida. The firm has even completed projects in Europe—including a luxuriously appointed yacht. The small, hands-on practice is led by Barbara, who works closely with her clients to set the design vision for every project. Assisting Barbara are Nicholas Lapp and a staff of five part- and full-time employees. The firm's diverse portfolio includes new and renovated residences and offices.

Barbara certainly has a rich career to reflect upon and a bright future to look forward to. She retains her philanthropic commitments to the museum world. However, private practice is the primary focus of this highly organized designer. Presently, she is working on design of waterfront homes in Westport and Palm Beach. Barbara sums up her practice succinctly: "Working with first-class architects and clients who understand art and design makes for amazing projects."

TOP LEFT
Sugimoto photographs hang above a tufted headboard in a luxurious master bedroom with a variety of textures.
Photograph by Phillip Ennis

BOTTOM LEFT
A Hamptons den using casual fabrics like chenille, leather and suede features a sofa tucked between built-in bookcases.
Photograph by Phillip Ennis

FACING PAGE
A large island topped in custom-colored turquoise lava stone echoes the glass tiles of the backsplash in a sleek country kitchen. Texture is provided by bamboo blinds at the windows.
Photograph by Phillip Ennis

MORE ABOUT BARBARA ...

WHAT IS THE HIGHEST COMPLIMENT YOU'VE RECEIVED PROFESSIONALLY?

To be asked by existing clients to do another project for them, and knowing the next one will be different. You are familiar with everything they have, so you are challenged to take them in a new direction.

WHAT IS THE MOST UNUSUAL/EXPENSIVE/DIFFICULT DESIGN OR TECHNIQUE YOU'VE USED IN ONE OF YOUR PROJECTS?

Working with French cabinetmakers who incorporate techniques not readily utilized in the United States, such as illuminated bookcase shelves that are completely adjustable without exposed wiring.

WHAT SINGLE THING WOULD YOU DO TO BRING A DULL HOUSE TO LIFE?

Incorporate contemporary art or photography; it doesn't have to be expensive, but art gives personality and interest to walls so the space feels complete.

WHAT IS THE BEST PART OF BEING AN INTERIOR DESIGNER?

There are two parts for me—the creative challenge at the beginning of a project, when I'm dealing with a "blank slate" and then seeing all the complex parts come together at the end.

ON WHAT PERSONAL INDULGENCE DO YOU SPEND THE MOST MONEY?

Collecting post-war and contemporary art and 20th-century French antiques.

BARBARA LANE INTERIOR DESIGN
Barbara Lane
2 East 67th Street
New York, NY 10021
212.737.2802

SUSSAN LARI

SUSSAN LARI ARCHITECT PC

In a pretty Persian accent tinged with emotion, architect Sussan Lari explains that good design has the power to shape people's lives. She has built her six-person practice around the full spectrum of design—from architecture, interiors, lighting and furniture to complete construction administration—coupled with exceptionally strong and collaborative relationships with her clients. Thirty years of professional experience have reinforced Sussan's philosophy that every project look different, to reflect its unique owners, site and context. "I take particular joy in designing homes that will impact the emotional and spiritual well-being of their occupants."

Sussan's projects look distinctly different; she does not embrace or promote a single aesthetic style, but instead emphasizes appropriate scale and proportion of volumes, attention to detail and use of natural materials and light. Careful siting of projects considers the relationship between landscape and house. "Just as you can't force a style of clothing onto a body that isn't appropriate, I won't force a style of design onto the land," she explains. Her interior designs tend to use unique applications of natural finish materials, for which she personally cooperates with installers and craftspeople. Playful combinations of wood and stone are juxtaposed with rich color schemes and a mix of classical and contemporary furnishings, many designed by Sussan herself.

Sussan's commitment to residential architecture follows a path of practical and professional leadership. After many years of work in corporate architecture and the birth of her daughter, she founded Sussan Lari Architect PC, in 1992. This offered her the flexibility of time with her own family, and the freedom to choose her clients. She soon realized that residential projects were her real passion.

ABOVE
The library of an off-Fifth Avenue loft—in lower Manhattan—is adjacent to the master bedroom.
Photograph by Peter Rymwid, www.PeterRymwid.com

FACING PAGE
The loft's library is also accessible from the living room. Behind the railing on the right, a raised platform houses the dining room and kitchen.
Photograph by Peter Rymwid, www.PeterRymwid.com

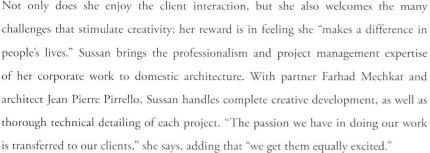

Not only does she enjoy the client interaction, but she also welcomes the many challenges that stimulate creativity; her reward is in feeling she "makes a difference in people's lives." Sussan brings the professionalism and project management expertise of her corporate work to domestic architecture. With partner Farhad Mechkat and architect Jean Pierre Pirrello, Sussan handles complete creative development, as well as thorough technical detailing of each project. "The passion we have in doing our work is transferred to our clients," she says, adding that "we get them equally excited."

Sussan has two master's degrees from the University of Pennsylvania: in urban design and in architecture, and an undergraduate degree from Tehran University in Iran. She has been active in the American Institute of Architects chapters in New York and Long Island, where she served as chapter president in 2000, and received a Board of Directors Award of Service recognizing her years of contributions and leadership.

Sussan's work is included in the book *Dream Homes Metro New York* and has been published locally and nationally.

ABOVE LEFT
Custom-designed cabinetry graces the den of a United Nations Plaza apartment in New York City.
Photograph by Peter Rymwid, www.PeterRymwid.com

ABOVE RIGHT
Cabinetry was added to the entrance of a United Nations Plaza apartment to create more privacy for the dining area.
Photograph by Peter Rymwid, www.PeterRymwid.com

FACING PAGE TOP
Fully gutted and redesigned, this historical townhouse in Upper East Side Manhattan has a second-floor living room, a balcony to the lower-floor breakfast area and a door to the garden.
Photograph by Peter Rymwid, www.PeterRymwid.com

FACING PAGE BOTTOM
The living room with a built-in bar leads to a casual sitting area.
Photograph by Peter Rymwid, www.PeterRymwid.com

JASPER JOHNS

MORE ABOUT SUSSAN ...

WHAT IS THE HIGHEST COMPLIMENT YOU'VE RECEIVED PROFESSIONALLY?

I really believe that good design can make a difference in people's comfort. The best compliments are when clients say they love their new home, and tell me they feel peaceful there, or when clients say they got something they never dreamed possible.

WHAT BOOK ARE YOU READING RIGHT NOW?

Social Intelligence: The New Science of Human Relationships by Daniel P. Goleman.

IF YOU COULD ELIMINATE ONE DESIGN/ARCHITECTURAL/BUILDING TECHNIQUE OR STYLE FROM THE WORLD, WHAT WOULD IT BE?

Deconstructivism.

WHAT ONE ELEMENT OF STYLE OR PHILOSOPHY HAVE YOU STUCK WITH FOR YEARS THAT STILL WORKS FOR YOU TODAY?

I use natural materials and light.

SUSSAN LARI ARCHITECT PC
Sussan Lari, AIA
31 Warner Avenue
Roslyn Heights, NY 11577
516.625.2916
www.sussanlari.com

Irving Penn PASSAGE

NEW HOPE FOR AMERICAN ART

BRUCE NORMAN LONG

BRUCE NORMAN LONG INTERIOR DESIGN

Bruce Norman Long wanted to be an interior designer for as long as he can remember, and feels fortunate to have made a successful career doing work that he loves. As a child, Bruce requested furniture for Christmas presents and drew floor plans in his free time. As a teen, his first design project was redecorating a portion of his family home. He credits his parents with encouraging this creative passion. They raised three sons in a house filled with antiques and artwork. Yet, instead of putting rooms and valuables off-limits, they encouraged a lifestyle of appreciation and comfort. Bruce grew up respecting the finest things in life—from art to family—and today designs spaces that foster this same level of livability and enjoyment within beautiful surroundings. "Every room should be used or I haven't done my job," he says, explaining that by listening carefully to his clients, he creates houses that are a reflection of their individuality.

LEFT
This view of the designer's own home in Bucks County shows a confident and eclectic mix of furnishings spanning a century of decorative arts. A large pair of French trumeau mirrors reflects the owner's collection of art.
Photograph by John Armich

181

Bruce brings a great deal of respect to his clients' preferences and budgets. "I love buying beautiful things for other people, but I respect their money and understand value," he explains. Appropriateness is his guiding design principle. "I like rooms with personality," he says, adding that what may be right for one client is not suitable for another. From formal to casual, the range of his designs speaks to his eclectic clientele in New Jersey and New York, and as far away as London, Santa Fe and Palm Beach.

A highly regarded interior designer whose work has been featured in *House Beautiful, British House & Garden, Design Times* and several books, Bruce believes his understanding of architecture is what sets him apart. Most of his projects include components of renovation or new construction, making them about much more than just decorating. His education and early professional experience combine for a background rich in classic proportions, balance and detail.

After earning a Bachelor of Fine Arts and a Bachelor of Interior Architecture from the Rhode Island School of Design, Bruce worked with renowned designer Mark Hampton for five years. He describes this experience—including interior design of the White House for President George and First Lady Barbara Bush—as extraordinary, and having profoundly influenced his career. He launched Bruce Norman Long Interior Design in 1993 and today has offices in both Princeton, New Jersey, and Manhattan.

Bruce is very involved in the arts community, and has participated in numerous showhouses, including the prestigious Vassar, Kips Bay and Princeton Showhouses. In his part-time residence of Bucks County, Pennsylvania, Bruce serves as president of the Phillips' Mill Community Association—the oldest arts organization in Bucks County—and is an avid collector of Bucks County Impressionist and Modernist art.

TOP LEFT
The living room has pale mossy-taupe cross striae walls and a sumptuous coral velvet sofa. Paisley pillow fabric is repeated on painted fauteuil. Painting by Glenn Harrington.
Photograph by John Armich

BOTTOM LEFT
Two bronze Dore lanterns illuminate a celadon dining room with custom mahogany table and chairs sitting on a rug from F.J. Hakimian.
Photograph by John Armich

FACING PAGE LEFT
This Riverside Drive apartment was designed in pale tones to complement the stunning view. A pair of club chairs by Donghia are opposite a slipper chair from Roman Thomas. Polished nickel lamps are from Jerry Pair.
Photograph © image / dennis krukowski

FACING PAGE RIGHT
A custom-designed aluminum desk with an automobile finish sits centrally in a study at the Kips Bay Showhouse. The large watercolor is by Paul Ching-Bor.
Photograph © image / dennis krukowski

More About Bruce ...

WHAT IS THE HIGHEST COMPLIMENT YOU'VE RECEIVED PROFESSIONALLY?

Every "thank you" is a huge compliment and being called again for future projects is even better.

WHAT IS THE MOST UNIQUE/IMPRESSIVE/BEAUTIFUL HOME YOU'VE SEEN AND WHY?

I recently saw a modern prefab house in the desert near Palm Springs; it was beautifully detailed with a great floor plan and fantastic site. It felt very livable.

WHAT COLOR BEST DESCRIBES YOU AND WHY?

French blue-grey-green; it is extremely versatile, classic, timeless, modern or antique.

WHO HAS HAD THE BIGGEST INFLUENCE ON YOUR CAREER?

Mark Hampton and my parents.

BRUCE NORMAN LONG INTERIOR DESIGN
Bruce Norman Long
136 East 57th Street, Suite 1705
New York, NY 10022
212.980.9311
www.bnl-interiordesign.com

32 Nassau Street, Fourth Floor
Princeton, NJ 08540
609.921.1401

SUSAN LUSTIK

SUSAN LUSTIK, INC.

Susan Lustik's creative background is as richly textured as one of her room designs. She studied at The Julliard School's pre-college division, earned undergraduate and graduate degrees in French from Queens College and Tufts University, respectively, and taught the subject to high school and college students. During a research fellowship, she traveled extensively throughout Europe studying Renaissance design and decorative arts. Mentor and friend Harvey Rosenberg encouraged her to pursue decorating as a career choice, so Susan enrolled in Parsons School of Design. In 1983, upon completing her studies, she began her namesake interior design business. In more than two decades of practice, Susan has earned a reputation for working closely with her clients, and for being able to capture their spirit within rooms that are both comfortable and beautiful.

Most of Susan's designs are traditional in style; however, she has also completed contemporary homes. The thread of commonality woven through her work is an emphasis on creating houses that are appropriate for—and expressive of—the people who live there. "I believe in a strong collaborative effort between designer and client so that, as we go through the design process together, the best decisions are made for the project, both aesthetically and practically," she explains. Susan abides by three basic design principles: comfort, functionality with adaptability and the best possible quality. "My footprints should be invisible," she believes.

When Susan was selected to participate in a Long Island "Gold Coast" designer showhouse, her attention to detail and commitment to capturing family spirit was clear. She reinterpreted her room in the 1918 house-museum to imagine how the original family would live today. The curatorial staff was so impressed with Susan's concept that they opened the museum archives and allowed her to accessorize the space with the family's personal items.

ABOVE
The living room fireplace, an original architectural detail in this 1926 Connecticut home, is now the focal point around which family and friends gather in a room filled with comfortable seating, antiques and family treasures.
Photograph by Bill Rothschild

FACING PAGE
The Robert Chanler murals in this 1918 Long Island mansion inspired Susan to blend the original owners' elegant Gold Coast lifestyle with their passion for the rugged American West. Cowhide armchairs and Remington bronzes contrast with luxury fabrics and antique silver for this showhouse.
Photograph by Bill Rothschild

Often working in older houses, Susan is mindful of existing architecture, and incorporates appropriate detailing so that her work blends seamlessly. "In my opinion, architecture is the one art form that everyone interacts with on a daily basis," she explains. She extends this commitment to architectural integrity to her public service efforts. Susan has been involved as an advocate and facilitator for several Long Island communities' programs to revitalize their downtowns and restore a sense of charm and character by rethinking "big box" and "strip mall" retail in favor of thoughtful community planning. Susan also is an allied member of the American Society of Interior Designers and a member of the Institute for Classical Architecture and Classical America and the American Friends of the Georgian Group.

Projects by Susan Lustik have been featured in *House* magazine and the *Times Beacon Record* newspapers.

LEFT
Once a loggia in this 1910 waterfront estate on Long Island, the designer transformed the original concrete floor and stucco walls into a handsome and functional paneled office.
Photograph by Bill Rothschild

FACING PAGE LEFT
A Federal-style mirror reflects the comfortable and inviting dining room in this period home. The fresh colors of the walls, fabrics and custom rug update the traditional look.
Photograph by Bill Rothschild

FACING PAGE RIGHT
A colorful Empire-style rug anchors this sun-filled entry hall where the antique chandelier and mirror add sparkle. A comfortable bench and the soft glow of pale yellow walls welcome visitors.
Photograph by Bill Rothschild

MORE ABOUT SUSAN ...

WHAT ONE ELEMENT OF STYLE OR PHILOSOPHY HAVE YOU STUCK WITH FOR YEARS THAT STILL WORKS FOR YOU TODAY?

Listen closely to clients, understand them completely and capture their spirit in the designs, creating rooms that are comfortable and intimate for family use, yet adaptable and welcoming for entertaining.

WHAT IS THE MOST UNIQUE/IMPRESSIVE/BEAUTIFUL HOME YOU'VE SEEN AND WHY?

Rosecliff in Newport, Rhode Island; the Stanford White masterpiece is an American Beaux Arts model of restrained opulence.

WHAT IS THE MOST UNUSUAL/EXPENSIVE/DIFFICULT DESIGN OR TECHNIQUE YOU'VE USED IN ONE OF YOUR PROJECTS?

I designed an apartment for a client with advanced multiple sclerosis. Because the client—an enormously intelligent and sophisticated woman—is confined to a wheelchair, most of the furniture had to be custom designed with her physical limitations in mind, all the while maintaining a cohesive design vision. The project required a lot of patience and attention to detail.

WHAT IS THE HIGHEST COMPLIMENT YOU'VE RECEIVED PROFESSIONALLY?

When a client becomes a friend.

SUSAN LUSTIK, INC.
Susan Lustik
245 East 87th Street
New York, NY 10128
212.348.8260
www.susanlustikinc.com

MICHAEL MARIOTTI
MICHAEL MARIOTTI INTERIOR DESIGN

According to interior designer Michael Mariotti, quality of life and happiness go hand-in-hand with a well-designed home. "If you are comfortable in your environment, then you will be better equipped to face life's challenges," he strongly believes. While Michael's clients have different criteria for their houses, the interior designer's common thread is his ability to make each home a reflection of the client's best qualities. His philosophy and approach create homes that are smart, inspiring and ultimately functional.

Assisted by a staff of three, Michael is personally responsible for each project's design vision. After meeting with clients to understand their needs and preferences, he develops the interior, and often exterior, concepts. He applies his "classic style with a modern twist" to balance functionality and timelessness. His own recently constructed home, which he designed reminiscent of a French château, is often complimented by people who say it looks as if it has always been there.

As concerns for the environment have increased, so has Michael's inclusion of eco-sensitive products and finishes with naturally aesthetic qualities. Bamboo and cork flooring, natural textiles and recycled tile have been incorporated into recent projects. Energy-efficient LED lighting is also regularly used in conjunction with ample natural light.

Attention to detail, sophisticated color palettes and elegant styling are hallmarks of the firm's work. Custom furniture designs cater to clients' exacting needs. Michael's expertise in lighting design has resulted in stunning use of light, such as in one kitchen, where a cove ceiling was clad in tin and illuminated by xenon lights; the design makes the entire ceiling glow with warmth.

ABOVE
A dominance of simple shapes and a relatively monochromatic color scheme give the traditional pieces in this family room a modern edge.
Photograph by Sasha Nialla Photography

FACING PAGE
The convex, antiqued mirror creates a casual yet elegant focal point for a formal dining room that adjoins a kitchen.
Photograph by Sasha Nialla Photography

From an early age, Michael has been known for his motivation and energy. As a senior in high school, he worked part-time for a design firm. The job nurtured his passion and proficiency for design. His employers also recognized his talent, sponsoring him in a variety of pre-college courses at prestigious New York design schools. Michael went on to earn an interior design degree from Parsons School of Design, which included significant coursework in lighting design. He founded Michael Mariotti Interior Design in 1987, and has since completed high-end residential and commercial projects in the metropolitan area and across the country. Michael is a professional member of the American Society of Interior Designers and an associate member of both the International Association of Lighting Designers and the National Kitchen and Bath Association. His projects have been featured in *New York Spaces*, *New Jersey Monthly* and *Showhouse*, a book of showhouse designs from across the country.

Michael's approach is grounded in the belief that "good synergies produce good outcomes." His enthusiastic and friendly nature instills confidence in clients. Ultimately, these strong relationships build rewarding working experiences and beautiful homes.

TOP LEFT
An eclectic mix of juxtaposing shapes and sizes as well as various materials brings interest to this modern living room.
Photograph by Sasha Nialla Photography

BOTTOM LEFT
The touches of bold, acid green in this living room add a fresh pop of color to the quiet hues of brown.
Photograph by Phillip Ennis Photography

FACING PAGE
This Country French-style kitchen is appointed with traditional elements yet has current components like stainless steel appliances and a contemporary chandelier.
Photograph by Phillip Ennis Photography

MORE ABOUT MICHAEL ...

ON WHAT PERSONAL INDULGENCE DO YOU SPEND THE MOST MONEY?

Travel; experiencing the world inspires creativity.

WHAT COLOR BEST DESCRIBES YOU AND WHY?

Blue; to me it represents water, sky and endless possibilities.

WHO HAS HAD THE BIGGEST INFLUENCE ON YOUR CAREER?

My father, David; he always supported my dreams and taught me to follow them. He said, "The less you let fear bog you down, the more goals you'll be able to accomplish."

WHAT DO YOU LIKE ABOUT PRACTICING IN YOUR LOCALE?

Working in New York is the ultimate trade resource.

MICHAEL MARIOTTI INTERIOR DESIGN
Michael Mariotti
979 Third Avenue, Suite 2C
New York, NY 10022
212.753.2220
www.michaelmariotti.com

CHRISTOPHER MAYA

CHRISTOPHER MAYA, INC.

"Shouldn't your home be a place you want to be?" asks Christopher Maya. The interior designer creates comfortable, welcoming environments that make his clients love their houses. His comprehensive approach emphasizes details, history and open lines of communication. He values each client's input and could not imagine designing a room without this personal dialogue. Christopher enjoys helping clients understand what their vision of home really is. "It is so gratifying to help people articulate what they really want and to translate what they visualize into something real."

He has no qualms about designing for big families, numerous pets or active lifestyles. His ultimate goal is to make people's lives more relaxed in an otherwise chaotic and complicated world. Subtle patterns and textures, soothing colors and natural materials work together with classical design elements to achieve a look that never appears trendy, and yet always fits the pace of modern life.

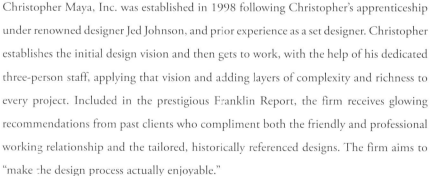

Christopher Maya, Inc. was established in 1998 following Christopher's apprenticeship under renowned designer Jed Johnson, and prior experience as a set designer. Christopher establishes the initial design vision and then gets to work, with the help of his dedicated three-person staff, applying that vision and adding layers of complexity and richness to every project. Included in the prestigious Franklin Report, the firm receives glowing recommendations from past clients who compliment both the friendly and professional working relationship and the tailored, historically referenced designs. The firm aims to "make the design process actually enjoyable."

Christopher gets his inspiration from art and architectural history. He performs a tremendous amount of research for every project, developing a "visual vocabulary" to help communicate design ideas to his clients. The Parsons School of Design-educated Christopher studied oil painting, infusing his work with a strong sense of color and texture. He also collects furniture and artwork from all periods. This combined appreciation and understanding of fine art coupled with his penchant for history results in designs that are timelessly original.

Christopher's signature brand of understated elegance has been featured in *House Beautiful*, *Metropolitan Home* and *Martha Stewart Living* and included in the Lee Jofa promotional catalog. He has participated in the Kips Bay Decorator Show House and the *Hamptons Cottages & Gardens* Idea House. Recently, the firm donated design services for the restoration of an antique house in Westport, Connecticut, as part of a project being undertaken by the Westport Historic District Commission. In work ranging from new construction to historic preservation, Christopher proves that comfort and sophistication can be beautifully combined.

MORE ABOUT
CHRISTOPHER ...

WHAT IS THE HIGHEST COMPLIMENT YOU'VE RECEIVED PROFESSIONALLY?

It is always a compliment when clients tell me how much they continue to enjoy living in their homes year after year. It's testimony to the timeless appeal that I strive to achieve in my work.

WHAT ONE ELEMENT OF STYLE OR PHILOSOPHY HAVE YOU STUCK WITH FOR YEARS THAT STILL WORKS FOR YOU TODAY?

Rooms should flow into one another with ease and there should be continuity between architecture and color throughout the home.

ON WHAT PERSONAL INDULGENCES DO YOU SPEND THE MOST MONEY?

Furniture and art.

WHAT BOOKS HAVE HAD THE GREATEST IMPACT ON YOU?

The Moon and Sixpence by W. Somerset Maugham, based on the life of artist Paul Gauguin.

The Grass Harp by Truman Capote. I always loved the brilliantly inspired imagery in this book of stories.

CHRISTOPHER MAYA, INC.
Christopher Maya
60 East 66th Street, Suite 3b
New York, NY 10021
212.772.2480
www.christophermayainc.com

RUSSELL MINION
JUAN CARLOS
GUTIERREZ

MINION - GUTIERREZ DESIGN

The average homeowner might find the potential challenges of a design and construction project overwhelming. Russell Minion and Juan Carlos Gutierrez—the two principals of Minion-Gutierrez Design in Manhattan—aim to dispel any fear and encourage clients to embrace the potential of good design. "The possibility of creating a space and the sense of accomplishment when the client is happy are the best parts of being a designer," explains Russell.

Minion-Gutierrez Design is known for understated elegance, with spaces that are filled with light and enhanced by refined architectural detailing. Their client-focused philosophy is summarized succinctly by Russell, "We take care of whatever happens during the process, and we always keep our clients happy." Their approach is one of collaboration, with each other and with their clients, to create spaces that are efficient, cohesive and always tailored to each client's personality and lifestyle.

Just as Russell and Juan Carlos enjoy collaborating with their clients, they work together on every project. "We complement one another," says Juan Carlos, an architect with 20 years of professional experience, including 10 in his native Colombia. He holds an architectural degree from the Pontificia Universidad

Javeriana in Bogotá. Russell spent three years at the New York School of Interior Design before leaving to begin his practice in 1996. Juan Carlos joined him in 2000. Their combination of architecture and interior design skills, enhanced by frequent travel abroad for inspiration, lends an international panache to every project. They are assisted by a staff of two.

Russell and Juan Carlos begin an assignment by asking clients to describe their preferences using adjectives—traditional, modern, English, French, chic, classic—that help shape their design. Then the required spatial needs and functionality are overlaid. Juan Carlos describes their role as artists interpreting the lifestyle of every client. Often, the design process is a learning experience, as the two partners teach their patrons about different products and material qualities. Their work is never cookie-cutter, but instead displays a remarkable range of aesthetics, from beach house casual to uptown sophistication.

Occasionally, the adjective approach presents unanticipated results. For the home featured here, the clients described preferences for English, French and Spanish architecture as well as angles. Russell and Juan Carlos combined the styles, giving each room in the house its own unique personality, yet with an interconnected feel. It is a clear demonstration of how every design is customized to client needs and preferences.

Both partners speak to the benefits of good design, and advocate fine architectural detailing and good lighting over an excess of furniture or decorative elements. "A room that is well-lit with nice detail may look just perfect with a few chairs, it doesn't need more. We never overdecorate," says Russell.

Russell and Juan Carlos bring a passion to their work, aiming to create spaces that are appropriate for the people who will live there. They suggest anyone who is beginning a project seek a designer with similar enthusiasm. "If you look for passion in your designer, you know they will execute a job the best they can," believes Juan Carlos.

Minion-Gutierrez Design has been featured in *Design NJ*, *Food & Wine* and *Array* magazines.

More about Russell & Juan Carlos ...

RUSSELL, WHAT IS THE MOST UNIQUE/IMPRESSIVE/BEAUTIFUL HOME YOU'VE SEEN AND WHY?

Castle Drogo by architect Edwin Lutyens; it is an impressive building but on the inside it feels intimate.

JUAN CARLOS, WHAT BOOK HAS HAD THE GREATEST IMPACT ON YOU?

Love in the Time of Cholera by Gabriel Garcia Márquez.

ON WHAT PERSONAL INDULGENCE DO YOU SPEND THE MOST MONEY?

Travel; it gives us inspiration and knowledge of architecture and design around the world.

WHAT ONE ELEMENT OF STYLE OR PHILOSOPHY HAVE YOU STUCK WITH FOR YEARS THAT STILL WORKS FOR YOU TODAY?

Keep the clients happy no matter what.

MINION - GUTIERREZ DESIGN
Russell Minion
Juan Carlos Gutierrez
347 Fifth Avenue, Suite 1307
New York, NY 10016
212.545.7846
www.miniongutierrez.com

ADRIENNE NEFF

ADRIENNE NEFF DESIGN SERVICES, LLC

Many designers describe comfort as a key part of a successful interior. Adrienne Neff understands the importance of marrying comfort with sophistication, to ensure the homes she designs are appropriate for both casual family relaxation and formal entertaining. In fact, her greatest compliment came when a client admitted the first thing he did in his newly designed space was to fall asleep in front of the television, beer in hand. "He felt at home right away," Adrienne recounts. "The day-to-day moments in your house should be enjoyable." Adrienne's knowledge of 20th-century decorative arts and her penchant for timeless, classic décor enrich her comfortable interior designs with eclecticism and elegance.

Founded in 2004, Adrienne Neff Design Services, LLC, draws upon Adrienne's experiences working with interior and product designer Thomas O'Brien, architect Alan Wanzenberg, and antiques dealers Liz O'Brien. While each of those style arbiters deeply influenced her aesthetics and way of doing business, Adrienne credits her clients with providing the greatest inspiration. "Each project is a collaborative effort. There is a lot of trust involved," she explains. "My best clients are receptive to new ideas that enrich their tastes and views of design. They challenge me and bring out the best in me."

Adrienne is known for detail-oriented interiors that engage all of the senses. She thinks about texture in a variety of situations—the sensation of carpet on bare feet or the feel of a sofa against bare legs. She works with light to create moods and to illuminate specific tasks, such as reading or dining. Color, patterns and always fresh flowers are used to enliven rooms. Passionate about her ideas, Adrienne is also committed to reliability and responsiveness. Her attention to details ensures her clients' needs and concerns—whether large or small—are always addressed. "I serve as my clients' advocate so that every detail is executed to perfection," she adds.

ABOVE
The bowl's narrow, brown concentric circles stand in stark contrast to the simple yet elegant white tea set.
Photograph by John R. Gruen

FACING PAGE
Floral patterns adorning the walls of this Manhattan apartment's master bedroom are accentuated by the vibrant flower-patterned pillow.
Photograph by John R. Gruen

Adrienne earned a Bachelor of Arts in English and philosophy from Barnard College at Columbia University. Always interested in art and design, she was awarded a Merit Scholarship to the prestigious Sotheby's American Arts Course, a one-year certificate program focusing on American fine and decorative arts. Adrienne went on to study interior design at Parsons School of Design. She worked in the industry for a decade before founding her own firm. In addition to running her practice, the New York native is a member of the Institute for Classical Architecture and an enthusiastic collector of color photography. She was recently featured in *Domino* magazine and has appeared in three episodes of the NBC program "House Smarts."

MORE ABOUT ADRIENNE ...

WHAT IS THE BEST PART OF BEING A DESIGNER?

In the words of Austin Powers, "Freedom, baby!"—freedom to design new projects, freedom to explore design concepts and freedom to grow personally and professionally.

WHAT ONE ELEMENT OF STYLE OR PHILOSOPHY HAVE YOU STUCK WITH FOR YEARS THAT STILL WORKS FOR YOU TODAY?

"God is in the details," Mies van der Rohe. The best designers will lovingly take the time to thoughtfully create a space made up of a minutia of details—the binding on a carpet, the trim on a pillow, the paint finish. In the right hands, all of these seemingly mundane details will add up to a unique, dynamic and engagingly tactile environment.

WHAT IS A SINGLE THING YOU WOULD DO TO BRING A DULL HOUSE TO LIFE?

Add generous amounts of fresh flowers. They lift our moods and stimulate the senses with their scents, textures and colors each season. They clue us in to enjoy the moment right now.

WHAT BOOK ARE YOU READING RIGHT NOW?

White Walls: Collected Stories by Tatyana Tolstaya.

ADRIENNE NEFF DESIGN SERVICES, LLC
Adrienne Neff
191 Grand Street, Suite 3
New York, NY 10013
646.613.8460
www.adrienneneff.com

AMANDA NISBET

AMANDA NISBET DESIGN, INC.

With interiors noted for color, comfort and elegance, the work of Amanda Nisbet Design, Inc. has been called cheerful and unpretentious. "I want my clients to come home and be happy," the designer explains. Amanda oversees a staff of three who are committed to collaborative client relationships and balancing good design with a smooth business operation. In practice since 1998, Nisbet and her firm have been widely covered in House & Garden, Home, Elle Décor, Quest, Traditional Home and Town & Country magazines, as well as The New York Times and The Washington Post. They have completed projects across the United States, in Canada and in Europe. Supplementing her interior designs, Amanda offers a line of home accessories, some of which are featured in the Vivre catalogue.

Born in Montreal, Amanda moved to the United States when she was 14. Her circuitous path to design evolved from a variety of informal studies—art history, Italian, architecture and design—in the United States and Italy. Influenced by her mother, an avid amateur decorator, and her sister, a classically trained designer, Amanda has absorbed the careful balance between rule-making and rule-breaking.

Her work displays a fresh approach to classical design, emphasizing clean lines, bright colors and space planning that is sensitive to both children and adults. As such, she has become a favorite of families looking for sophisticated, elegant spaces that also feel comfortable for day-to-day living.

Amanda has a what-you-see-is-what-you-get attitude that puts her clients at ease. "Working with an interior designer is a big investment and an intimate process," she describes. "I want my clients to feel a sense of trust." Amanda believes helping her clients enjoy the process is critical to giving them a home best suited to their lifestyle and needs. The mother of two young children, Amanda understands the importance of a home that looks stylish, but feels relaxed.

Amanda is also committed to a number of charity organizations, including the Memorial Sloan-Kettering Cancer Center. She has participated in the highly regarded Kips Bay Decorator Show House and the *House & Garden* Hampton Designer Show House. Textile company Scalamandre selected Amanda as one of 25 designers to upholster a chair for their opening benefit.

While she lacks a trademark "look," her work always has an "easy elegance" defined by the jovial use of color, texture and line in sophisticated, yet surprising combinations. "You bring such joy to everything you touch," exclaimed one client. With her characteristic enthusiasm, Amanda says she looks forward to the challenge of each new project. "There are pros and cons to every project; I always learn something new." She makes it clear that there is nothing trivial about helping families create a sense of home.

MORE ABOUT AMANDA ...

WHAT IS THE BEST PART OF BEING A DESIGNER?

Always being on the hunt; I love searching for objects that can transform a room.

WHAT COLOR BEST DESCRIBES YOU AND WHY?

Pink; it is happy, vibrant and glam.

WHAT IS A SINGLE THING YOU WOULD DO TO BRING A DULL HOUSE TO LIFE?

Paint; it is the most efficient and inexpensive way to change a room.

WHEN YOU ARE NOT DESIGNING, WHERE CAN YOU BE FOUND?

With my children.

AMANDA NISBET DESIGN, INC.
Amanda Nisbet
1326 Madison Avenue, Suite 64
New York, NY 10128
212.860.9133
www.amandanisbetdesign.com

BARBARA OSTROM
BARBARA OSTROM ASSOCIATES

Barbara Ostrom Associates has a singular goal in mind—to create uplifting, inviting environments. Since 1977, the six-person interior decorating firm has been designing an eclectic range of high-end residential, commercial, restaurant and retail spaces for clients worldwide.

Principal Barbara Ostrom works carefully with every client to achieve their individual vision. For private residences, the aim is always to create warmth and comfort through colorful, energetic décor. "I don't ever want my work to be recognized," explains Barbara, "Every space represents the likes and dislikes and personality of the individual client."

Barbara finds that her clients tend toward a traditional blend of good antiques and classic furnishings. Her strength lies in layering color, texture and form to make the traditional appear energized and fresh. While she has completed projects in styles ranging from ultra-modern to Art Deco and everything in between, Barbara discourages clients from requesting period décor. Instead, she encourages the individuality and vibrancy that come from a mix of diverse furniture, artwork and decorative items. "Interior design has the power to make people joyful," she

exudes, adding that joy comes from spaces that are highly personalized rather than reproductions.

With more than 30 years as a designer, Barbara has the experience to support her convictions. She earned a Bachelor of Fine Arts from New York University and an interior design degree from the New York School of Interior Design. She also earned a Master of Science in Interior Design from Pratt Institute and a graduate certificate from the Sorbonne in Paris.

An avid reader, Barbara continues to educate herself about design through hundreds of books in her home and office. She has been personally recognized in more than 40 design books and in magazines ranging from *Robb Report* to *House & Garden*, as well as with a host of awards and inclusion on numerous "best of" lists.

ABOVE
The color palette is soft yet vibrant, giving this room a completely unique yet timeless style.
Photograph by Phillip Ennis

FACING PAGE
Every last detail has been thoughtfully considered and brilliantly executed in this bedroom suite.
Photograph by Phillip Ennis

Active professionally, Barbara is a member of the American Society of Interior Designers and has served on its board of directors, and she lectures frequently at New York design schools. She also serves on the advisory board of the New York School of Interior Design.

Barbara is proud of her ability to transform client dreams into reality every day. She recently completed the design of a New York restaurant where the client's enthusiasm stretched her imagination. For the interior of the Italian-themed restaurant, Barbara established the dining area as a two-level palazzo, complete with theater-quality lighting to transform the restaurant's interior from day to twilight to night. Restaurant amenities were disguised as mock storefronts along the lower level, with the wine cellar and meat locker appearing as charming shops around the plaza.

TOP LEFT
A classically inspired work of art hangs above the exquisite sofa, which is upholstered in a striking, striped fabric.
Photograph by Phillip Ennis

BOTTOM LEFT
From ceiling to floor, this light-infused living space demonstrates a keen attention to detail.
Photograph by Phillip Ennis

FACING PAGE LEFT
Custom design motifs bring this kitchen to life.
Photograph by Phillip Ennis

FACING PAGE RIGHT
The residents' cherished collection of dishes is highlighted in the custom-built cabinet.
Photograph by Phillip Ennis

Barbara's residential work incorporates similar creativity and attention to every detail. From a carefully painted trompe l'oeil ceiling that looks like a garden trellis to intricately crafted custom cabinetry, Barbara's designs consider every surface. Spaces are alive with color and character at every turn.

Immersing herself in the client's lifestyle is part of what makes Barbara enjoy her profession, and what makes her portfolio so diverse. Barbara's wide range of clients has included President and Mrs. Richard Nixon, Russell and Kimora Lee Simmons and Senator and Mrs. Gerard Cardinale. Barbara Ostrom Associates has completed projects in the New York metropolitan area and across the United States, in the Caribbean and in Europe.

ABOVE LEFT
Rich wood paneling lends an intimate feel to this space, while the globe mural directs attention upward.
Photograph by Phillip Ennis

ABOVE RIGHT
The voluminous ceiling is punctuated by deeply stained beams and a soothing green wall color.
Photograph by Phillip Ennis

FACING PAGE LEFT
Bathed in natural light, this relaxation area is replete with a piano and a variety of seating options.
Photograph by Phillip Ennis

FACING PAGE RIGHT
The residents' love of card games is cleverly demonstrated on the ceiling, which is a nice complement to the well-established, sophisticated ambience of the rest of the room.
Photograph by Phillip Ennis

MORE ABOUT BARBARA ...

WHAT IS THE BEST PART OF BEING A DESIGNER?

My clients; the ability to help put someone's dreams into actuality makes us both happy.

ON WHAT PERSONAL INDULGENCE DO YOU SPEND THE MOST MONEY?

I collect antique Chinese foo dogs.

WHAT DO YOU LIKE ABOUT PRACTICING IN YOUR LOCALE?

There is a great variety of houses—from city apartments to beachfront vacation homes to cabins in the mountains—that provides opportunities for different styles and approaches.

WHAT ONE ELEMENT OF STYLE OR PHILOSOPHY HAVE YOU STUCK WITH FOR YEARS THAT STILL WORKS FOR YOU TODAY?

No single element applies to all clients. People are different, and eclectic within themselves.

WHAT IS A SINGLE THING YOU WOULD DO TO BRING A DULL HOUSE TO LIFE?

Add color.

BARBARA OSTROM ASSOCIATES
Barbara Ostrom
1 International Boulevard, Suite 209
Mahwah, NJ 07495
201.529.0444

55 East 87th Street
New York, NY 10128
212.465.1808
www.barbaraostromassociates.com

DAVID SCOTT PARKER

DAVID SCOTT PARKER ARCHITECTS, LLC

A noted authority on American furniture, architect David Scott Parker not only manages his namesake firm, David Scott Parker Architects, LLC, but also co-owns Associated Artists, LLC, a Southport gallery specializing in decorative arts from the late 19th and early 20th centuries. Just as the turn of the last century was filled with exuberance, as formality began to recede and the aesthetic movement invigorated design with light and color, David's work demonstrates similar eclecticism and sense of surprise. His incorporation of personal items in combination with distinctive furnishings ensures his architecture and interiors retain intrinsic qualities of which one never grows tired. "Design should be a part of life, not a passing fad," he states.

Known for both new construction and historic restoration, David Scott Parker Architects, LLC has been designing architecture and interiors of private homes, museums and historic sites for the past two decades. Balancing their appreciation and knowledge of history and design with the collaborative input of each client, David and his firm have developed a portfolio of elegantly detailed projects. "I see design as an iterative process that first and foremost starts with the client," explains David. He creates both tension and balance between style, form, surface

and color, always aiming to express each client's unique personality within the space. As architect and interior designer, David is able to seamlessly integrate the two disciplines.

David knew he wanted to be an architect since attending a lecture at age 12 given by architectural historian and arts advocate Ralph Schwarz. He went on to earn a Bachelor of Science in architecture from the University of Virginia and a Master of Architecture from Harvard University. He also holds a Certificate in Interior Design from the University of Evansville in Indiana. After graduation, David worked for renowned modernist Richard Meier on projects including the J. Paul Getty Fine Arts Center in Los Angeles. The rigorous process and attention to detail he learned at Meier's firm continue to inform his practice today.

ABOVE
A new stair and bold herringbone floor are among the architectural details that updated this mid-19th-century Gramercy Park duplex.
Photograph by Mick Hales

FACING PAGE
Although their initial instinct was to replace the original Rococo mantel, the designer retained and balanced it with the owners' eclectic collection of personal artifacts and inherited furnishings.
Photograph by Mick Hales

David's commitment to design is shared by a staff of 18 including associate principal John Wasilewski. They firmly believe there is no single approach that is best for all clients, and tailor their services accordingly. Residential projects have been completed along the East Coast in addition to significant institutional commissions, including restorations at the U.S. Treasury in Washington, D.C., and numerous museums in the city of Bethlehem, Pennsylvania. David and the firm's work have been published in *House & Garden*, *Classic American Homes*, *The New York Observer* and *The New York Times*.

ABOVE
A Frankenthaler oil established the palette for this West Side pied-à-terre. It hangs adjacent to a 1940s' era eglomise screen. Light, color, form and reflection animate the space.
Photograph by Mick Hales

FACING PAGE
Atop an East Side 1882 brownstone David restored, the new rooftop conservatory incorporates antique leaded windows and a Tiffany fountain with a marble mosaic floor he designed.
Photograph by Mick Hales

MORE ABOUT DAVID ...

ON WHAT PERSONAL INDULGENCE DO YOU SPEND THE
MOST MONEY?

My library, which is an invaluable resource and also a wonderful retreat—except
that my need for books expands more quickly than shelf space.

WHAT BOOK HAS HAD THE GREATEST IMPACT ON YOU?

Italo Calvino's *Invisible Cities.*

WHAT ONE ELEMENT OF STYLE OR PHILOSOPHY HAVE YOU STUCK
WITH FOR YEARS THAT STILL WORKS FOR YOU TODAY?

Always invest in quality, quality, quality.

WHAT IS THE MOST UNIQUE/IMPRESSIVE/BEAUTIFUL HOME YOU'VE
SEEN AND WHY?

Sir John Soane's townhouse in London; it is a fabulous example of a period
eclectic interior that artfully expresses the personality and creative genius of its
acquisitive owner.

DAVID SCOTT PARKER ARCHITECTS, LLC
David Scott Parker, AIA
170 Pequot Avenue
Southport, CT 06890
203.259.3373
www.dsparker.com

SABIN PATTERSON
PAMELA BANKER ASSOCIATES

"To be a good designer, you need to create unique and individual looks for each client's lifestyle," explains Sabin Patterson. Believing that an eclectic space is a more interesting space, the interior designer encourages his clients to purchase items they love, invest in good artwork and embrace their own personal style. "My biggest challenge—and the best part of my job—is helping clients design homes that are uniquely theirs," he says. After operating his own firm, Patterson Design Group, Inc., for 10 years, Sabin joined Pamela Banker Associates in January 2007. The firm takes a classical approach to contemporary living.

"You don't want a house that looks like your neighbor's house," Sabin maintains. He brings a sense of inventiveness to his work, never afraid to incorporate color—chocolate brown is a favorite—or to juxtapose traditional and contemporary furnishings. Advocating appropriately scaled pieces and moderation, Sabin dissuades clients from over-accessorizing. Yet he always incorporates items that have personal or sentimental value, to make every home feel meaningful. His client relationships are open and intimate, resulting in projects that are not only beautiful, but are also comfortably livable.

One of Sabin's passions is collecting artwork, from recognizable names to up-and-comers. "I love the opportunity to introduce my clients to a new artist," says the designer, who spends much of his free time visiting galleries for fresh inspiration. He is also motivated by the vendors and craftspeople with whom he works. "They contribute pearls of wisdom to make my designs better."

Blending interior design with architecture is an objective and a strength of Pamela Banker Associates. Pamela has more than 30 years in the interior design business,

ABOVE
A view down the simple yet elegant gallery hall leading to the master bedroom.
Photograph courtesy of Pamela Banker Associates

FACING PAGE
Natural light illuminates the warm earth tones of this cozy living room overlooking Central Park.
Photograph courtesy of Pamela Banker Associates

including tenure at the acclaimed firm Parish-Hadley Associates. Her private residential, corporate and club designs in both the United States and England have graced the pages of *Architectural Digest* and *House & Garden*. Sabin brings his own portfolio of residences, restaurants and hotels, all of which are characterized by a consistent look of sophisticated timelessness. Recently called "sumptuous" and "glamorous" by *Washington Spaces* magazine, Sabin's work has also been featured in *The New York Times* and *Colorado Homes & Lifestyles*.

The regional influences and eclectic variety in Sabin's portfolio come from his experience working around the country. After attending the interior design program at the Colorado Institute of Art, he moved to Chicago and founded his firm. As he began to complete projects nationwide, he relocated to be nearer the design resources of the East Coast. Providing him access to galleries and vendors, and the proximity to sit sketching quietly by the beach, the New York region gives Sabin the inspiration to continue designing homes as unique and diverse as his clientele.

LEFT
Sublime craftsmanship is on display via the palatial table and decorative chair comprising the foyer.
Photograph courtesy of Pamela Banker Associates

FACING PAGE
Abundant wood paneling affords an engaging backdrop to this rich library/den.
Photograph courtesy of Pamela Banker Associates

MORE ABOUT SABIN ...

WHAT IS THE BEST PART OF BEING A DESIGNER?

Never knowing what type of project I'll be working on next; I love the challenge of helping any clients achieve what they want for their homes.

WHAT ELEMENT OF STYLE OR PHILOSOPHY HAVE YOU STUCK WITH FOR YEARS THAT STILL WORKS FOR YOU TODAY?

Less is more; you only need a few great pieces to make a huge statement.

WHAT COLOR BEST DESCRIBES YOU AND WHY?

Chocolate brown; it is warm and always in style.

WHAT IS A SINGLE THING YOU WOULD DO TO BRING A DULL HOUSE TO LIFE?

Paint; color is the best way to bring life to any style of house. Or, if all else fails, a martini will liven things up.

PAMELA BANKER ASSOCIATES
Sabin Patterson
136 East 57th Street, Fifth Floor
New York, NY 10022
212.308.5030
www.pamelabanker.com

CAMPION PLATT

CAMPION PLATT

Whether he is designing a custom residence, a home-away-from-home boutique hotel or a line of furniture, architect and interior designer Campion Platt has one thing in mind: luxury. "Luxury is about both materiality and context," he explains, adding that context might mean creating clear, open spaces within the confines of a Manhattan apartment, or selecting opulent finishes—such as leather, resin or marble—to accentuate spatial forms. Campion's ideas of luxury consistently incorporate fine craftsmanship and contemporary styling. For the past 20 years, Campion Platt has shown clients across the country how to make modern design both sophisticated and soothing.

Campion earned an undergraduate degree from the University of Michigan, and a Master of Architecture degree from Columbia University. A member of the American Institute of Architects and the Architectural League of New York, he understands the importance of creating architecture and interiors that meld seamlessly. His holistic approach creates highly personalized spaces—making him a favorite of celebrities including Al Pacino, Meg Ryan, Roger Waters and Conan

O'Brien. A full gamut of specialized artisans and craftspeople execute Campion's designs, which often incorporate new and innovative material uses.

Campion's staff of seven includes Design Director Heather Moore. Together, Moore and Campion conceptualize all of the interior designs. A brainstorming session at the start of each project asks the question, "What does this project want to be?" soliciting input from all staff members, as well as assessing parameters in a nearly forensic manner. Designs are dictated by extensive client-generated wish lists, rather than preconceived notions, resulting in a varied portfolio. "No two of our projects are the same," says Campion, who emphasizes contrasts in design and believes that his work is constantly evolving. The only element that consistently remains the same is a commitment to clean, fresh luxury.

ABOVE
The penthouse apartment's living room looks onto a terrace. Lucite steps and a glass rock moat separate the indoors from the outdoors.
Photograph by Campion Platt

FACING PAGE
An intimate seating area surrounds the unique coffee table.
Photograph by Campion Platt

The full-service firm has been a leader in boutique hotel design, setting benchmarks with such projects as the Mercer Hotel in New York and the Chateau Marmont Hotel in Hollywood—both of which Campion was also involved in as a co-developer—and Boston's Bulfinch Hotel. Recognition and accolades for Campion and the firm have been widespread, ranking on *Architectural Digest*'s "AD 100" list of the world's top interior designers and *New York Magazine*'s "The City's 100 Best Architects and Decorators," as well as publication in magazines from *Elle Décor*, *House & Garden* and *Gotham* to *Esquire* and *Travel & Leisure*.

To keep his design inspirations flowing, Campion travels frequently. While he appreciates the beauty of European cities such as Paris, he is most inspired by the simple, deliberate housing and lifestyles of Southeast Asia. "I like considering the translation to our own culture, and the free association of ideas." Always generating new ideas, Campion recently launched a custom furniture company to complement his architecture and interiors. From 19th-century campaign-style furniture to sleek modern pieces, the collections include the same sumptuous finishes and careful attention to proportion and detail. The firm has recently launched a fabric line with Jim Thompson and a hardware line with Nanz Hardware to continue the theme of modern luxury.

TOP LEFT
The Fifth Avenue pied-à-terre overlooks Central Park. Simple custom furniture is a pleasing juxtaposition against the wall of intricate millwork, which accommodates the client's art collection.
Photograph by Campion Platt

BOTTOM LEFT
Custom Platt designs—interlocking nesting tables in pickled ash, a club chair and a sofa—are complemented by the soft features of the antique screen.
Photograph by Campion Platt

FACING PAGE LEFT
A gunmetal-finished custom bar enclosure and walnut butcher block countertop beautifully frame the clients' image of a mountain range in South America.
Photograph by Campion Platt

FACING PAGE RIGHT
The hallway leading to the master bedroom boasts maple burl and cane panels. Side tables and lamps designed by Platt flank the focal point of the room—the bed, which has a large suede headboard panel edged with button details.
Photograph by Campion Platt

MORE ABOUT CAMPION ...

NAME ONE THING MOST PEOPLE DON'T KNOW ABOUT YOU.

I am a Buddhist.

WHAT IS THE MOST UNIQUE/IMPRESSIVE/BEAUTIFUL HOME YOU'VE SEEN AND WHY?

Any of the John Lautner-designed houses in Los Angeles; they are modern, totally free-form, majestic and personal, yet universal.

WHO HAS HAD THE BIGGEST INFLUENCE ON YOUR CAREER?

The Italian architect Carlo Scarpa (1906-1978). He was known for revising and editing drawings in numerous layers on a single sheet, and for his innovative use of materials. I also believe in the importance of material selection, craftsmanship and refinement.

WHAT ONE ELEMENT OF STYLE OR PHILOSOPHY HAVE YOU STUCK WITH FOR YEARS THAT STILL WORKS FOR YOU TODAY?

Make it luxurious.

CAMPION PLATT
Campion Platt, AIA
152 Madison Avenue
New York, NY 10016
212.779.3835
www.campionplatt.com

MARK ALAN POLO

POLO M.A., INC.

Designer Mark Alan Polo loves a challenge. "I'm not interested in sameness— at any level," he reveals. The veteran interior designer has spent the past 30 years stepping up to a host of challenges, from starting a design practice right out of college to creating interiors in a multitude of styles and locations across the country. With a penchant for "textural eclecticism" within pared-down traditional environments, and a philosophy based on collaboration and unpredictability, Mark has established himself as a passionate and committed designer.

Educated at Rutgers University School of Art and the New York School of Interior Design, Mark's entrepreneurial independence was clear from the earliest point in his career. After working for a reputable antiques dealer during school, Mark and a partner opened their own design business shortly after graduation. "There wasn't anyone to tell us what we were doing was 'wrong' and so our creativity was allowed to grow," he

remembers. Mark infused his projects with an appreciation of form and shape, and his knowledge of antiques. Although the partnership dissolved, Mark soon founded his current practice, Polo M.A., Inc. After 18 years in Fort Lee, the New Jersey town nearest to Manhattan, Mark longed for more space and relocated the office to Boonton, Morris County, New Jersey.

Polo M.A. includes a staff of four who assist with production and project support. Mark continues to establish the design direction and creative vision for each project. "On every level, I want some element of the unexpected," he describes. Unpredictable pairings, such as horse hair and Plexiglass in a traditional room, or a pop-up television within a double-back sofa, are the types of inclusions for which Mark and his firm have become known. Projects in an array of different aesthetics display Mark's diverse design skills. He believes people are inherently eclectic in their tastes and lives, and therefore, home designs should be an eclectic blend of complementary styles.

Polo works collaboratively with his clients, explaining "otherwise it becomes my house— and it's not." The process is a learning experience for both parties; clients learn to vocalize who they are through descriptions of their likes, dislikes, hobbies, entertaining styles and lifestyles. Mark enjoys what he calls the "layered exploration" where he uses the knowledge to generate personal, comfortable spaces. He believes a good working relationship is essential, explaining there is a "balance between ego and entertainment." He wants clients to share his excitement and enthusiasm with the creative process.

ABOVE LEFT & FACING PAGE
A fabulous Morristown, New Jersey, living room features a hand-colored "hombre" ceiling and a plasma television situated behind beautiful cabinetry, the equipment for which is installed in an antique Chinese cupboard.
Photograph by Phillip Ennis

ABOVE RIGHT
A period library in Englewood, New Jersey, evokes warmth, bringing the 21st century not only to the art and furnishings but also to communication. Television, music equipment and Internet access are brilliantly designed into the antique leather chaise and back of the mohair drop-arm sofa so that work and entertainment can coexist with traditional beauty.
Photograph by Phillip Ennis

Mark also works closely with architects, preferring to be involved in new construction projects as early as possible. This ensures a seamless integration of his interiors with the architectural design. A testament to his working relationships with other design professionals, Mark has been asked to decorate the home of an interior designer friend, and has been sent client referrals from designers who no longer practice in his region.

Always wanting his work to be fresh and different, Mark welcomes any design challenges, whether from a client's suggestion or from his own imagination. He has quarried stone from Israel for use as a project's flooring, envisioned elaborate wall murals and faux painting schemes and incorporated fine artwork. Antiques are selected for most projects. Mark's ability to blend form with function helped an indoor pool pavilion feel like an intimate spot for a swim or a spacious gathering area for parties. His suggestion to remove a bedroom from a client's home evolved into an elegant three-story staircase. The newness of each design project energizes him with fresh creativity.

Published regionally in *201*, *New Jersey Monthly*, *New Jersey Countryside* and *Hunterdon Life* magazines, Mark has also been published nationally in *House Beautiful*. He has earned accolades as one of the "Best of" Bergen and Morris County designers. His work has received two *New Jersey Monthly* design awards. He is an allied member of the American Society of Interior Designers and is a member of the International Interior Design Association.

MORE ABOUT MARK ...

WHAT IS THE BEST PART OF BEING A DESIGNER?

The challenge and the newness.

NAME ONE THING MOST PEOPLE DON'T KNOW ABOUT YOU.

I love to write, and have been working on a novel.

IF YOU COULD ELIMINATE ONE DESIGN/ARCHITECTURAL/BUILDING TECHNIQUE OR STYLE FROM THE WORLD, WHAT WOULD IT BE?

The split level.

WHO HAS HAD THE BIGGEST INFLUENCE ON YOUR CAREER?

Sister Parish and Jackson Pollock.

POLO M.A., INC.
Mark Alan Polo, IIDA, Allied Member ASID
310 Main Street
Boonton, NJ 07005
New York: 212.754.1844
New Jersey: 973.402.7400
www.polomainc.com

JENNIFER POST
JENNIFER POST DESIGN

Clients engage award-winning interior designer Jennifer Post for her ability to reconstruct entirely new living environments—in her signature contemporary style. "We only take on the niche clientele who basically want to go through a complete renovation or build a home from scratch," Jennifer describes of her eight-person firm's approach. This fresh start ensures interior architecture and interior design merge seamlessly. The elegantly minimal and light-filled results are a careful balance between stylish sophistication and extreme functionality.

For the self-described perfectionist, it is important that every Jennifer Post design is immaculately conceived, detailed and constructed. Unlike many other designers, Jennifer sketches, draws and documents each project personally, and her firm provides comprehensive construction management. Her study of architectural principles and her fine arts background combine for an approach that treats each home like a piece of artwork. Clear spatial organization along a primary axis is emphasized, as are balance, continuity and clarity of form. Color and texture are used in sublime moderation for a timeless effect. All work is characterized by an

abundance of natural light illuminating pure white walls to create an ethereal elegance Jennifer terms "classical contemporary." The sleek modernism is juxtaposed with luxurious finish materials—cashmere, silk and down—for a comfortable, livable warmth.

As disciplined and organized as her interiors, Jennifer works carefully with her high-end, sophisticated and high-energy clientele to ensure their homes are a reflection of their lifestyles. Jennifer is extremely dedicated to each client's vision, striving for perfection on every project she completes. While the interiors may appear minimal, each is exceptionally organized for functionality and practicality. Closets, bathrooms and kitchens are meticulously designed for adequate and appropriate storage. "The less clutter you have, the more elegant your home can look," Jennifer believes.

ABOVE
This New York residence features sliding glass panels—like interior windows—that link the media and dining rooms and extend the views of Central Park. Kara Walker artwork adorns the left wall.
Photograph by Antoine Bootz

FACING PAGE
Neutral tones of this New York city living room are enlivened by Russell Sharon's colorful artwork and sleek chairs by Holly Hunt.
Photograph by Antoine Bootz

Jennifer founded her eponymous firm in 1991 and has since completed projects across the country and internationally. The practice has evolved into one of the top spatial design firms in the country, providing a complete range of services from architecture and interior design to full-scale construction management to the total selection of all interiors. Jennifer Post Design presently maintains offices in New York, Palm Beach and Los Angeles. Called "immaculate" and "most progressive," the firm's work has been covered in *The New York Times* and all the major shelter magazines, including *House & Garden, Elle Décor, Metropolitan Home* and *The Robb Report*.

"I want my clients to appreciate their lives more after my work is done," Jennifer explains; this enthusiasm for architecture and interiors has resulted in numerous repeat clients. In fact, she has been recommissioned for clients' second homes without fail.

The level of trust clients grant her to develop their vision—and their reliance upon her to execute that vision—are her greatest compliments. Jennifer is passionate about her work—and about how good design can influence lifestyle, earning her repeat inclusion on *Architectural Digest*'s coveted "AD 100" list of the world's top architects and designers.

Jennifer believes simplicity is the key to successful interior design, and abides by architect Mies van der Rohe's famous adage "less is more." Just as Mies was a pioneer in early 20th-century modernism, Jennifer has established herself as one of the leading interior designers of her time.

MORE ABOUT JENNIFER ...

WHAT COLOR BEST DESCRIBES YOU AND WHY?

White; to me it represents purity, freedom and order.

WHAT ONE ELEMENT OF STYLE OR PHILOSOPHY HAVE YOU STUCK
WITH FOR YEARS THAT STILL WORKS FOR YOU TODAY?

Simplicity.

WHAT DO YOU LIKE BEST ABOUT BEING AN INTERIOR DESIGNER?

The joy and discipline of creating and making people feel overjoyed with their home.

ON WHAT PERSONAL INDULGENCES DO YOU SPEND THE
MOST MONEY?

Abstract art acquisitions and travel.

Photograph by Robert Whitman

JENNIFER POST DESIGN
Jennifer Post
25 East 67th Street, Suite 4A
New York, NY 10021
212.734.7994
www.jenniferpostdesign.com

239

RANDALL RIDLESS

RANDALL A. RIDLESS, LLC

Interior designer Randall Ridless clearly recalls the most stylish home he ever visited; it was owned by late French decorator Henri Samuel. The authentic 18th-century Parisian house was furnished in an eclectic mix of items from the 18th through 20th centuries. "The whole house was very chic, without the seriousness of any one period," Randall explains. He and his eight-person design firm bring similar classic, timeless style to an impressive portfolio of retail and residential work, describing their approach as a "loosened-up take on traditional."

After spending 13 years directing store design for Macy's, Bloomingdale's and Sak's Fifth Avenue, Randall formed his own design practice eight years ago. With vice president Beth Martell, who oversees the firm's residential work, Randall A. Ridless, LLC has completed luxury retail and custom residential projects around the globe, including the international store re-imaging program for Burberry and the interiors of the Saint Andrews Grand Club—overlooking the famed Royal and Ancient Golf Course—in Scotland.

Randall combines his years of design and construction management experience with an appreciation for art and architectural history. "My office has walls of books,

and I'm always buying new ones," he says of the collection, which offers inspiration and reference. This love of history comes in handy for developing store designs that exemplify a brand's past, and it also demonstrates Randall's commitment to learning as much as he can about every client. The firm works collaboratively with residential clients, understanding each family's unique differences and how their lifestyles should be reflected in the design and décor of their homes.

Designs are notable not only for appropriateness but also for beautiful detailing. Randall, who earned a BFA from the Rhode Island School of Design for industrial and furniture design, integrates into his projects custom furniture, textiles and rugs.

Color is used inventively, often in monochromatic schemes with neutral accents. Texture plays a critical role, in unexpected options such as "cat-scratch" velvets or thick linens. "We often take a fabric and have a pattern custom-embroidered," describes Randall, who loves the subtlety of creating a "signature stripe." Antiques mixed with contemporary pieces complete the firm's eclectic and youthful brand of traditional that has won wide acclaim.

House & Garden named Randall one of the 10 designers to watch for the 21st century. *House Beautiful* has recognized him as one of America's top 100 designers for the past eight years in a row. Magazines including *Gotham*, *New York* and *Interior Design* have also included him in their lists of top designers.

MORE ABOUT RANDALL ...

WHAT IS THE BEST PART OF BEING A DESIGNER?

Hands-down, it is the diversity of people you meet and how the work changes from day to day and year to year.

WHAT ONE ELEMENT OF STYLE OR PHILOSOPHY HAVE YOU STUCK WITH FOR YEARS THAT STILL WORKS FOR YOU TODAY?

Appropriateness; I listen to my clients as much as possible to give back their fantasies, made even better.

WHAT BOOKS HAVE HAD THE GREATEST IMPACT ON YOU?

The House in Good Taste by Elsie de Wolfe and *The Decoration of Houses* by Edith Wharton; the ideas of both still hold true today.

WHAT IS A SINGLE THING YOU WOULD DO TO BRING A DULL HOUSE TO LIFE?

Color is your friend—a can of paint can so dramatically change a dull room or a dull house.

RANDALL A. RIDLESS, LLC
Randall Ridless
315 West 39th Street, Suite 1104
New York, NY 10018
212.643.8140
www.randallridless.com

JENNIFER RUSCH
STUART NAROFSKY

WAYS2DESIGN AND NAROFSKY ARCHITECTURE

When the New York Institute of Technology launched its "We Create Dreams" advertising campaign, it did more than promote architectural education. The models selected were architect Stuart Narofsky, then professor of architecture, and recently graduated designer Jennifer Rusch. The two formed a friendship that evolved into marriage and a thriving design collaboration. Their practices, Narofsky Architecture and ways2design, joined together in 2004 to provide seamlessly integrated architecture, interiors and furniture design services. "We consider ourselves one firm."

Both partners believe that "architecture should push your senses." Their philosophy is for detail-oriented, well-thought-out designs that balance aesthetics with practicality. Contemporary architectural forms are complemented by warm natural materials and ultimately livable interiors. Through texture, color and sight lines, every space becomes a layered composition.

Jennifer and Stuart are members of the U.S. Green Building Council and are working towards LEED (Leadership in Energy and Environmental Design) accreditation. They consider their office Green in its approach and design solutions.

Their commitment to environmental responsibility begins with respect for a project's site. Sun studies and appropriateness of materials, forms and scale to both natural and man-made landscape are carefully considered. "Most of what we do has sustainability in mind," Stuart says, describing recent projects that have incorporated photovoltaic solar power and water reclamation systems, as well as recycled and renewable finishes. "We combine smart design with the use of health-friendly materials," he adds.

Jennifer elaborates on materials usage, explaining that she is conscious of long-term maintenance and durability. "I like a home you don't have to worry about," she says. By using durable materials—ceramic tile is a favorite—in unique ways, she balances aesthetics with practicality.

ABOVE
Industrial materials, such as stainless steel and glass, cohabitate with wood panels, textured fabrics and leather. The modern style is unified without sacrificing warmth.

FACING PAGE
Different functions of this 2,500-square-foot open space are integrated by a colored band of origami with public areas in the center and private spaces at either end.
Photographs by Phillip Ennis

She describes the powder room as an often-overlooked opportunity for creativity. "The room should be interesting and inviting—after all, it is a room most of your guests will visit." Jennifer has created custom wood sinks with hidden drains, and custom faucets. Her consideration of simple elements, like hiding trash cans from sight, makes spaces appear clean and stylish without disrupting functionality.

Jennifer and Stuart balance their family and work by living in an apartment adjacent to the office. Based in the Flatiron District of Manhattan, they are surrounded by resources and inspirations. Each credits the other's influence with enhancing the creative process. "There is constant dialogue every day," Jennifer explains. The conversation includes clients, who are very much involved. Each finished project strives for a careful balance of satisfied programmatic needs, site-appropriate architectural forms and inspired interiors.

The work of ways2design and Narofsky Architecture has been featured in *Distinction, Newsday Home* and *Residential Architect* magazines and in the book *Dream Homes Metro New York*.

MORE ABOUT JENNIFER ...

ON WHAT PERSONAL INDULGENCE DO YOU SPEND THE MOST MONEY?

Food; I love to cook.

WHAT IS THE BEST PART OF BEING A DESIGNER?

I have the opportunity to make a home what it should be—a place you never want to leave and that you want everyone to visit.

IF YOU COULD ELIMINATE ONE DESIGN/ ARCHITECTURAL/BUILDING TECHNIQUE OR STYLE FROM THE WORLD, WHAT WOULD IT BE?

Postmodernism.

WHAT IS THE MOST UNIQUE/IMPRESSIVE/ BEAUTIFUL PIECE OF ARCHITECTURE YOU'VE SEEN AND WHY?

The Jewish Museum in Berlin by Liebskind; it is important and influential and its spaces were able to affect me.

WAYS2DESIGN AND NAROFSKY ARCHITECTURE
Jennifer Rusch
Stuart Narofsky, AIA
4 West 22nd Street
New York, NY 10010
212.675.2374
www.ways2design.com

SANDRA SCHNEIDER

SANDRA STEELE SCHNEIDER INTERIORS

"Classic design never goes out of style," believes Sandra Schneider. Her balance of traditional styling with tasteful contemporary touches imbues her work with a timeless sophistication. No matter how formal a room's décor, Sandra advocates comfort. "I always include comfortable chairs, a place to set a drink and a spot to put up one's feet," she says. After all, a home is meant to be lived in—and comfort is key to a happy life. "I love being able to take a space and a client's things and transform them into someplace comfortable yet beautiful," she says. The designer particularly relishes any opportunity to incorporate prized client possessions. "It's more fun than a clean slate," she believes. From art collections to a grandmother's armoire, if something has sentimental value, Sandra will find a way to weave it into her design. The resulting projects are unique reflections of each client, interpreted by her namesake firm, Sandra Steele Schneider Interiors.

Sandra founded the firm in 1997 following a 10-year partnership in Vanderpoel Schneider Interiors. Although she has studied at the New York School of Interior Design, Sandra is largely self-taught. Her first career was in real estate, but her love of decorating and avid reading about design—and the encouragement of many friends and neighbors who solicited her creative talents—eventually led to her career change. Inspired by the likes of Sister Parish and Mark Hampton, Sandra is known for exceptional detailing, elegant window treatments and use of color. She avoids what is trendy, preferring instead to integrate today's interest in a cleaner, less fussy look with traditional details.

Assisting Sandra are office manager Cristina Bloise and design assistant Haley McGowan. Haley, also Sandra's daughter, followed her mother into the design business following a career in finance. Clients agree her innate creativity and enthusiasm match her mother's and keep the firm energized.

Sandra has participated in the prestigious Kips Bay Decorator Show House three times, and has twice designed a room for the organization's miniature rooms auction. She is a member of the Decorators Club of New York, and active in the Chamber of Commerce and Junior League of Bronxville. Her work has been published in *Avenue*, *Architectural Digest Brazil*, *Classic Home*, *Colonial Homes*, *Hamptons*, *Traditional Home*, *Westchester Magazine* and in several books. With projects ranging from the New York region to Vermont, Illinois, Florida, and even Switzerland, Sandra looks forward to her next design challenge, wherever it may take her.

TOP LEFT
French doors were installed to replace a window, providing better flow for entertaining on the patio, which is adjacent to the dining room of this Fleetwood, New York, residence.
Photograph by Sean Michael McGowan

BOTTOM LEFT
The walls of this Bronxville, New York, home's entrance hall were hand painted with a three-level tromp l'oeil scene that incorporates trees and architecture reflective of the Hudson Valley area.
Photograph by Sean Michael McGowan

FACING PAGE
The residents wanted to incorporate their treasured antiques and accessories while achieving a more contemporary look for their Fleetwood, New York, home.
Photograph by Sean Michael McGowan

MORE ABOUT SANDRA ...

WHAT COLOR BEST DESCRIBES YOU AND WHY?

Blue; it is one of nature's fabulous colors, with so many tones for all moods.

WHAT BOOK HAS HAD THE GREATEST IMPACT ON YOU?

The Fountainhead by Ayn Rand.

ON WHAT PERSONAL INDULGENCE DO YOU SPEND THE MOST MONEY?

Jewelry or books.

IF YOU COULD ELIMINATE ONE DESIGN/ARCHITECTURAL/BUILDING TECHNIQUE OR STYLE FROM THE WORLD, WHAT WOULD IT BE?

Mid-century modern; it just doesn't have the warmth of other styles.

SANDRA STEELE SCHNEIDER
Sandra Steele Schneider Interiors
70 Burkewood Road
Mount Vernon, NY 10552
914.668.4468
www.sandischneider.com

GAIL SHIELDS-MILLER
SHIELDS & COMPANY INTERIORS

The adage "like mother, like daughter" is one Gail Shields-Miller did not expect to live up to—at least not professionally. Despite being raised around her mother's successful design practice, Gail vowed not to become a designer. Yet after earning degrees in an unrelated field, she could not deny her penchant for the arts. An avid painter, sculptor and home decorator, she eventually pursued an interior design course of study at Parsons School of Design and opened her own firm. Today, she has reached a level in the industry where she is a highly respected and acclaimed designer amongst her peers, and has a clientele throughout the United States.

Shields & Company Interiors is recognized for its ability to mix design styles with beauty, comfort and elements of the unexpected. The firm works in both traditional and contemporary aesthetics, and will often combine the two—a classical apartment with modern furniture, for example. Gail emphasizes the way architecture and interiors work together to create a home's ambience. "You need to set the scene before you furnish it," she describes. Decorative mouldings, an exceptional paint job and appropriate lighting all add to the planning of rooms, which becomes the stage

for placing furniture and accessories. Gail is proud that her projects always have a stamp of her personality—a favorite color such as tomato red or an accent such as an antique Korean wedding chest—that might be found in her own house. Her sense of scale, color and detail is always used to complement the personality and preferences of her clients. The resulting homes are full of unpredictable elegance perfectly suited to every client.

Shields & Company's professional staff works closely with clients and craftsmen to ensure personal attention and high-quality results. Gail encourages her clients to be patient and enjoy the fluid, often-changing design process. She adds, "The homes we create make reference to a glamorous past, yet feel as if they are on the cutting edge of today's design trends, and are the results of our careful attention to detail and aesthetics. All of this requires time, cooperation and respect between the client and the designer."

Projects designed by Shields & Company have been featured in *Architectural Digest*, *New York Magazine*, *The New York Times*, *Interior Design* and more than a dozen books. In addition to her practice, Gail is an allied member of the American Society of Interior Design and the International Interior Design Association, and is an active member of the Institute of Classical Architecture, the Museum of Art and Design and the Museum for Women in the Arts.

TOP LEFT
Oversized walnut mouldings enhance the architectural details of this pied-à-terre in New York City. An original horn and rosewood-based dining table is located beside an oversized silver-leaf mirror to create a feeling of spaciousness.
Photograph by Michael Stratton

BOTTOM LEFT
In this apartment living room, a chocolate brown and cream color palette is spiked with cerulean blue and tomato red for interest. Two Andy Warhol lithographs hang above the custom sofa.
Photograph by Michael Stratton

FACING PAGE LEFT
Stainless steel barn doors, Venetian plaster walls and an original dining room table of African bubinga wood and bronze provide an inviting setting for entertaining guests.
Photograph by Michael Stratton

FACING PAGE RIGHT
Italian recliner chairs from the 1960s, an African bed and a one-of-a-kind orange pony skin horn chair sit playfully with other pieces of furniture in this eclectic Fire Island, New York, living room.
Photograph by Michael Stratton

MORE ABOUT GAIL ...

NAME ONE THING MOST PEOPLE DON'T KNOW ABOUT YOU.

I spent two weeks white water rafting in the Grand Canyon with nothing more than a Swiss army knife and a dry pair of socks—no makeup, no cell phone, no paint charts— and it was one of the most glorious times of my life. Skydiving is next!

WHAT DO YOU LIKE ABOUT PRACTICING IN YOUR LOCALE?

The New York market is inundated with whatever a designer needs. There are numerous talented artisans and creative companies that offer outstanding and unique products for designers to use.

ON WHAT PERSONAL INDULGENCE DO YOU SPEND THE MOST MONEY?

I have to confess that I am a travel junkie! I am determined to see each and every corner of the world; the more exotic, the more appeal a place has for me.

WHAT IS A SINGLE THING YOU WOULD DO TO BRING A DULL HOUSE TO LIFE?

An exceptional paint job by top-quality painters—the one thing so many clients devalue in the design process.

SHIELDS & COMPANY INTERIORS
Gail Shields-Miller, Allied Member ASID
149 Madison Avenue, Suite 201
New York, NY 10016
212.679.9130
www.shieldsinteriors.com

a little breathing room

cheryl terrace
vital design ltd

CHERYL TERRACE

VITAL DESIGN, LTD.

As the first eco-designer to participate in the renowned Kips Bay Decorator Show House, Cheryl Terrace created a remarkable "living" wall of greenery. The refreshing burst of oxygen that emanated from the live plants made many visitors ask if an air purifier was hidden inside. "Plants are air purifiers," Cheryl informed them with a smile. Her good-natured demeanor and casual attitude put people at ease. "Information and awareness are the most important parts of my design," she explains. Once people learn the benefits of living Green, they often could not imagine living any other way. She herself is a vegetarian, a yogi and a self-described "nature freak," but the houses she designs are the essence of elegant, luxurious living. If anyone has found a way to balance concern for the environment with concentration on the finer things in life, it is Cheryl.

Cheryl's sole proprietorship interiors practice, Vital Design, Ltd., was founded in 1997. A graduate of the New York School of Interior Design, Cheryl is guided by traditional design education infused with her interests in sustainable, responsible materials and systems. Her style is pure and organic, advocating a clutter-free, stress-free house that appeals to all the senses. "I love showing people that they do not need to sacrifice luxury or beauty to be environmentally thoughtful," she says.

More than just a decorator of physical space, Cheryl is about creating rooms that enhance her clients' emotional lives. Surrounding clients with things that make them happy—and that are good for them as well—involves selecting non-toxic paints; incorporating live plants, music and scent; and ridding spaces of clutter. Cheryl says every project is about listening to her clients' unique needs and creating spaces that work for them. "Good design can improve your quality of life," she advocates, explaining her belief that people are all interconnected. "By designing thoughtfully, we honor the connection between people and to the planet."

As Green design has hit mainstream media, many publications have taken notice of Cheryl. Her work has been featured in *Domino*, *Robb Report*, *In Style* and *Interiors*. She is negotiating a book deal to describe her philosophy and design approach to more readers and will soon host an eco-entertainment television show.

French playwright Jean Anouilh said, "Things are beautiful if you love them." Cheryl has made a career out of combining the beautiful things her clients love with comfort, warmth and genuine concern for the world. The results are stunning not only for their physical beauty but also for the transformative effects they have on clients. As Cheryl explains of both her company and her philosophy, "Vital Design has the unique ability to combine healthy design practices along with the fundamental understanding that home is where the soul is nurtured."

MORE ABOUT CHERYL ...

WHAT IS THE BEST PART OF BEING AN INTERIOR DESIGNER?

Seeing an incorrigible space transform into something beautiful is always wonderfully endearing—much like a person—but witnessing a client's life enhanced by that transformation is magical, and to me, deeply gratifying.

WHAT DO YOU LIKE MOST ABOUT DOING BUSINESS IN YOUR LOCALE?

My unique talent is bringing another dimension—a healthy environment—to a home. It has no specific locale or boundary but is about opening one's mind to the possibilities. The connection of mind, body and spirit reflects one's real home—one's heart.

IF YOU COULD ELIMINATE ONE DESIGN/ARCHITECTURAL/BUILDING TECHNIQUE OR STYLE FROM THE WORLD, WHAT WOULD IT BE?

Contrived, status-oriented, superficial style where the emphasis is on the price tag, not anything else.

VITAL DESIGN, LTD.
Cheryl Terrace
102 West 85th Street, #2G
New York, NY 10024
212.799.1540
www.vitaldesignltd.com

VICTORIA VANDAMM

VANDAMM INTERIORS

"Each room should be a masterpiece," believes interior designer Victoria Vandamm, whose four-person practice, Vandamm Interiors, provides residential and commercial design in New York, across the United States and in Europe. Victoria is a likeable, down-to-earth designer who is as comfortable with small-size or small-budget projects as she is with larger-scale efforts. In practice for nearly 30 years, Victoria is known for using the subtleties of light and the vibrancy of color to infuse houses with a freshness that transcends style or time.

"My job is to bring out the character of my clients, and express how they want to live," says Victoria. She enjoys stretching her creativity on projects ranging from houses to hotels to private yachts. An art major in college, Victoria owned a retail shop and provided interior decorating services before transitioning to full-time interior design in 1991. A self-described fanatic for color, texture and line, Victoria uses her skills to unify each project's architecture with each client's individual decorating and lifestyle.

Victoria's work expresses her awareness of light, from capturing the most sunlight to maximizing the glow of artificial lighting. She skillfully uses task and mood lighting to complement color schemes within a home and the environment seen through a home's windows. Her use of color is bold without being overwhelming, often in unexpected, edgy combinations or with strategically placed mirrors for added depth and reflection. Victoria believes rooms should be alive and involved with color, displaying a flirtatious, youthful quality that echoes between color, texture and client personality. "I don't want to stamp a project with my personal style," she promises. "I want it to belong to the person who lives there."

Victoria has been told she has an uncanny ability to conceptualize a project before putting pen to paper. Although she has completed numerous showhouse rooms—for Greenwich's Merrywood Designer Show House and Albert Hadley's Rooms with a View, among others—Vandamm prefers the constraints of real-life design challenges, with clients, budgets and preferences to incorporate.

ABOVE
This room is rich with the tones inspired by Roberto Cavalli's "Dark Lady" carpet. The silk ball gown draperies with crystal tassels are exquisite against the damask upholstered walls.
Photograph by Christopher Kolk

FACING PAGE
Opulent elegance and versatile dining: an intimate small table or seating for 24. Metallic wallpaper carries the glow of candlelight throughout the room. The table setting is by Trevor LaMarche.
Photograph by Kevin S. Dailey

"I like making all of the pieces fit," she explains, adding that "you don't have to spend a fortune to have a really good look." She advocates singular standout pieces and simplicity for smaller spaces or budgets, for example, a few exquisite accent tiles within a bathroom or one stunning piece of artwork in a living area. She also includes the element of surprise—something that "tweaks the visual tastebuds"—to make each room special.

Victoria's creativity is matched only by her professionalism. A board member of the Lockwood-Mathews Mansion Museum, she has chaired its annual garden and antiques shows. Her designs have been featured in *The New York Times*, *Connecticut Cottages and Gardens*, *Fairfield County Home*, *Greenwich Magazine*, *American Home Style* and *At Home*.

LEFT
The design highlights the warmth of Swedish antiques with a contemporary mix of textures and warm colors—silks against woods, crystal sparkling on Venetian plaster.
Photograph by Kevin S. Dailey

FACING PAGE TOP
This blue and white inspired bedroom features a crystal chandelier and a Victoria Vandamm-designed rug, combining the most favorite tones within the surrounding fabrics.
Photograph by Kevin S. Dailey

FACING PAGE BOTTOM
Using lavender as the neutral, a modern art collection lives happily amongst assorted antiques. Color and texture creates the constant flow throughout the room.
Photograph by Kevin S. Dailey

More about Victoria ...

WHAT BOOK ARE YOU READING RIGHT NOW?

The World is Flat: A Brief History of the Twenty-First Century by Thomas L. Friedman.

WHAT IS THE MOST BEAUTIFUL OR IMPRESSIVE HOME YOU'VE SEEN?

Buckingham Palace.

WHAT DO YOU LIKE ABOUT PRACTICING IN NEW YORK?

I love the energy of New York.

WHAT SINGLE THING WOULD YOU DO TO BRING A DULL HOUSE TO LIFE?

Use a few standout items to add interest.

WHAT COLORS BEST DESCRIBE YOU AND WHY?

Raspberry and aqua. One is happy and warm, and the other calm and cool. I love the juxtaposition.

VANDAMM INTERIORS
Victoria Vandamm
22A West Putnam Avenue
Greenwich, CT 06830
203.622.9070
www.vandamminteriors.net

TRISHA WILSON
WILSON ASSOCIATES

Trisha Wilson's first home was a hotel in Augusta, Georgia, where her father was manager and she was born. Little did she know that her destiny was already written in the stars. Today, Trisha is a world-renowned hotel designer—and truly a legend in her own right—whose extraordinary creativity, exceptional business savvy and work ethic are both unsurpassed and celebrated.

After graduating from the University of Texas with a bachelor's degree in interior design, Trisha began her career as a residential interior designer, and then took on restaurant design as a new challenge. With experience in these venues, she held her breath and took a giant leap forward into the world of hotel design. The famed interior architectural designer admits that she had some lucky breaks in her career, along with a little chutzpah for good measure. Renowned developer Trammel Crow Sr. gave her the opportunity of a lifetime that catapulted her into the world of hospitality: the chance to design her first hotel, the Loew's Anatole Hotel in Dallas—now the Wyndham Anatole.

She built her firm from the ground up, and over the past three decades, Wilson Associates has continued to flourish. Today, her company boasts nearly 300 employees, with its headquarters in Dallas and additional offices in New York, Los Angeles, Singapore, Shanghai, Johannesburg and Cochin. Trisha's firm routinely has 150 projects—from luxury hotels to restaurants and private residences—simultaneously underway around the globe.

With about 125 registered architects on staff, Trisha emphasizes architecture in all of her designs, which are driven by clients' needs, visions and financial parameters. She and her team pride themselves on not having a signature look to their work—rather, each project has a style that resonates with its client—though Trisha personally enjoys combining varied periods and styles.

Her firm's New York office, established in 1981, is led by longtime friend and talented designer Margaret McMahon. Though Margaret majored in political science, she simply could not deny her innate artistic talents and, through her mother's encouragement, set out to explore a variety of fields, completing her journey at her first destination. Margaret began her relationship with Wilson Associates as a temporary employee, immediately connected with the firm's culture and was so inspired by her experience that she went back to school to study design. She has been with the company ever since.

Together, Margaret and Trisha have embarked on dozens of projects, including Andre Agassi and Stefanie Graf's Fairmont Tamarack Resort in Idaho. As it was their first development project since retiring from the professional tennis world, Andre and Stefanie took a very personal approach to the project, thinking of it as a residence; the designers responded in kind by meeting with them in the comfort of their living room.

Margaret and Trisha feel that there are endless similarities between high-end resort and residential design, as patrons of the former universally seem to desire for their guests the personal quality of the latter. The knowledge gleaned from one type of project certainly informs the next. Though the challenges—physical and emotional—of one residential project are equal to several large-scale commercial projects, Trisha and her entire team agree that nothing compares to the joy of knowing people are living happily in one of their creations.

With the benefit of a striking percentage of repeat clients, Trisha and her team are willing to travel anywhere in the world that good design is needed—and their clients have taken them to nearly every continent. Forever guileless, Trisha always accomplishes what seems to be the impossible. Whether it is a splendid private residence in Manhattan, a funky in-crowd bar in Bangkok or a luxurious five-star resort hotel in Dubai, she maintains her simple yet effective philosophy: Tackle every design project one room at a time.

ABOVE
The owner's personal collection of African masks serves as a focal point for this welcoming media room.
Photograph by Michael Wilson

FACING PAGE
This study features a collection of antiques gathered from the owner's travels throughout the world.
Photograph by Michael Wilson

MORE ABOUT TRISHA ...

WHAT IS THE MOST VALUABLE THING YOU'VE LEARNED OVER THE YEARS?

I believe it's important to maintain an attitude of gratitude. In a service business like ours, we are all interdependent. I am grateful for the teamwork, creativity and commitment of my associates and for the tremendous projects our clients entrust us with—projects that take us to all corners of the world, places of incredible beauty and luxury.

WHAT ARE YOU PASSIONATE ABOUT?

The Palace of the Lost City introduced me to South Africa, and I have been in love with the country ever since. I became very concerned about the effects of poverty, HIV/AIDS, and lack of decent education for the children of South Africa, so I created The Wilson Foundation and focused my efforts around the town of Mabatlane, located in the Limpopo Province of South Africa. With help from my friends and colleagues in the design industry and elsewhere, The Wilson Foundation raises money to support programs and projects that bring a brighter future to so many individuals in this community. My passion is making a difference, one child at a time!

IF YOU WEREN'T AN INTERIOR DESIGNER, WHAT WOULD YOU BE DOING?

I'd be a professional cowgirl or a tap dancer.

HOW DO FRIENDS DESCRIBE YOU?

Honest. They know I will always say exactly what I think.

WILSON ASSOCIATES
Trisha Wilson, ASID
475 Park Avenue South, 23rd Floor
New York, NY 10016
212.213.1181
Fax: 212.213.1501
www.wilsonassoc.com
www.thewilsonfoundation.org

VICENTE WOLF

VICENTE WOLF ASSOCIATES, INC.

Vicente Wolf is quick to point out that he is more than a designer. He is also a professional photographer, a writer and a world traveler. "It's a broad range of interests and energy that makes me who I am as a creative person," he explains. While his creativity has an array of influences and outlets, it is through interior design that Vicente has made a name for himself. His 10-person design firm, Vicente Wolf Associates, Inc., has been in practice for upwards of 30 years, generating minimalist and refined interiors for residences and commercial spaces around the world. Marked by a clean mixture of different period elements accentuating their architectural backgrounds, Vicente's designs feature a painterly use of color and shifting views altered by light, texture and reflection.

The firm's signature style often incorporates a white or neutral background to enhance interior architecture and the furnishings within each space. Eclecticism and comfort guide every project. "We approach each job anew," Vicente describes, adding that the most wonderful part of design is the creative process. He likens his compositions to carefully arranged food on a white plate, and explains that his approach is architectural as opposed to decorative. In fact, Vicente has registered architects on staff, to carry his design vision across all facets of a project. In 1999,

Vicente opened VW Home, a retail store and showroom of furniture and accessories acquired on his world travels. Vicente also has several lines of custom-designed textiles, furniture and accessories.

Self-trained as a designer, Vicente turns to his extensive travels as a source for inspiration. "Understanding the world in a global way lets me think outside the box of New York City," he explains. He spent his childhood in Cuba, where his family's construction business influenced his appreciation for craftsmanship. His adulthood has included travel to some of the most primitive spots on the earth. This international perspective influences how Vicente selects and mixes objects. In two books on design, *Crossing Boundaries: A Global Vision of Design* and *Learning to See: Bringing the World Around You Into Your Home*, Vicente has championed his creative, intellectual approach.

ABOVE
The custom dining table and vases complement the light, color and mood of the client's painting.
Photograph by Vicente Wolf

FACING PAGE
This living room was designed to function as a formal space for entertaining guests, as well as a comfortable family room and library, with a sense of continuity created by the use of color throughout.
Photograph by Vicente Wolf

Vicente explains that his "passion for design is guided by the principles of integrity and simplicity." He and his work have been featured in national shelter media, including *Elle Décor, Interior Design, Veranda, House & Garden, Traditional Home* and *The New York Times. House Beautiful* recognized him as one of the ten most influential designers, and both *Architectural Digest* and *Metropolitan Home* have included him on lists of the 100 best designers.

TOP LEFT
The kitchen opens directly into the dining room. Three types of dining chairs and "Paris" stools at the island are available through VW Home, Inc. Custom designed by Vicente Wolf, the island has mahogany legs, stainless steel panels and a stainless steel top.
Photograph by Vicente Wolf

BOTTOM LEFT
Vicente Wolf designed the L-shaped sofa, which wraps around a Swedish birch armchair that dates between 1784 and 1818.
Photograph by Vicente Wolf

FACING PAGE LEFT
The custom upholstered headboard is flanked by a Vicente Wolf-designed night table with a Shagreen top and parchment drawer. Walls are upholstered in blue Bergamo "Samsar" silk.
Photograph by Vicente Wolf

FACING PAGE RIGHT
A mahogany, high-gloss lacquered vanity, designed by Vicente Wolf, possesses louver doors, stainless steel legs and a marble top.
Photograph by Vicente Wolf

MORE ABOUT VICENTE ...

ON WHAT PERSONAL INDULGENCE DO YOU SPEND THE
MOST MONEY?

Photography.

WHAT IS THE HIGHEST COMPLIMENT YOU'VE RECEIVED
PROFESSIONALLY?

The respect of my peers.

IF YOU COULD ELIMINATE ONE DESIGN/ARCHITECTURAL/BUILDING
TECHNIQUE OR STYLE FROM THE WORLD, WHAT WOULD IT BE?

Victorian; I think it lacks a sense of balance and scale.

WHAT IS THE MOST UNIQUE/IMPRESSIVE/BEAUTIFUL HOME YOU'VE
SEEN AND WHY?

A monastery in Bhutan; it had a palpable quality of peacefulness. It said so much with a
minimal amount of objects.

VICENTE WOLF ASSOCIATES, INC.
Vicente Wolf
333 West 39th Street
New York, NY 10018
212.465.0590
www.vicentewolfassociates.com

PUBLISHING TEAM

Brian G. Carabet, Publisher
John A. Shand, Publisher
Phil Reavis, Executive Publisher
Paul Geiger, Senior Associate Publisher

Beth Benton, Director of Development & Design
Julia Hoover, Director of Book Marketing & Distribution
Elizabeth Gionta, Editorial Development Specialist

Michele Cunningham-Scott, Art Director
Emily Kattan, Senior Graphic Designer
Ben Quintanilla, Senior Graphic Designer
Jonathan Fehr, Graphic Designer

Rosalie Z. Wilson, Managing Editor
Katrina Autem, Editor
Amanda Bray, Editor
Lauren Castelli, Editor
Anita M. Kasmar, Editor
Ryan Parr, Editor
Daniel Reid, Editor

Kristy Randall, Managing Production Coordinator
Laura Greenwood, Production Coordinator
Jennifer Lenhart, Production Coordinator
Jessica Adams, Traffic Coordinator

Carol Kendall, Administrative Manager
Beverly Smith, Administrative Assistant
Carissa Jackson, Administrative Assistant
Amanda Mathers, Sales Support Coordinator

PANACHE PARTNERS, LLC
CORPORATE OFFICE
13747 Montfort Drive, Suite 100
Dallas, TX 75240
972.661.9884
www.panache.com

New York Office
917.301.8716

Robin Key Landscape Design, *page 149*

THE PANACHE PORTFOLIO

Dream Homes Series

Dream Homes of Texas
Dream Homes South Florida
Dream Homes Colorado
Dream Homes Metro New York
Dream Homes Greater Philadelphia
Dream Homes New Jersey
Dream Homes Florida
Dream Homes Southwest
Dream Homes Northern California
Dream Homes the Carolinas
Dream Homes Georgia
Dream Homes Chicago
Dream Homes Southern California
Dream Homes Washington, D.C.
Dream Homes Deserts
Dream Homes Pacific Northwest
Dream Homes Minnesota
Dream Homes Ohio & Pennsylvania
Dream Homes California Central Coast
Dream Homes New England
Dream Homes Los Angeles
Dream Homes Michigan
Dream Homes Tennessee

Additional Titles

Spectacular Hotels
Spectacular Golf of Texas
Spectacular Golf of Colorado
Spectacular Restaurants of Texas
Elite Portfolios
Spectacular Wineries of Napa Valley

City by Design Series

City by Design Dallas
City by Design Atlanta
City by Design San Francisco Bay Area
City by Design Pittsburgh
City by Design Chicago
City by Design Charlotte
City by Design Phoenix, Tucson & Albuquerque
City by Design Denver
City by Design Orlando

Perspectives on Design Series

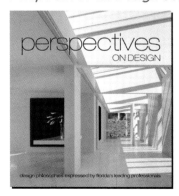

Perspectives on Design Florida

Spectacular Homes Series

Spectacular Homes of Texas
Spectacular Homes of Georgia
Spectacular Homes of South Florida
Spectacular Homes of Tennessee
Spectacular Homes of the Pacific Northwest
Spectacular Homes of Greater Philadelphia
Spectacular Homes of the Southwest
Spectacular Homes of Colorado
Spectacular Homes of the Carolinas
Spectacular Homes of Florida
Spectacular Homes of California
Spectacular Homes of Michigan
Spectacular Homes of the Heartland
Spectacular Homes of Chicago
Spectacular Homes of Washington, D.C.
Spectacular Homes of Ohio & Pennsylvania
Spectacular Homes of Minnesota
Spectacular Homes of New England
Spectacular Homes of New York
Spectacular Homes of Vancouver
Spectacular Homes of London

Visit www.panache.com or call
972.661.9884

PANACHE PARTNERS, LLC

Creators of Spectacular Publications for
Discerning Readers

INDEX